Faithful Interpretation

FAITHFUL
INTERPRETATION

Reading the Bible
in a Postmodern World

A. K. M. Adam

Fortress Press  Minneapolis

FAITHFUL INTERPRETATION
Reading the Bible in a Postmodern World

Cover image: © Royalty-Free/Corbis
Cover design: Brad Norr
Book design: Abby Hartman

Library of Congress Cataloging-in-Publication Data

Adam, A. K. M. (Andrew Keith Malcolm), 1957-
 Faithful interpretation : reading the Bible in a postmodern world
/ by A.K.M. Adam.
  p. cm.
 Includes bibliographical references and index.
 ISBN-13: 978-0-8006-3787-3 (alk. paper)
 ISBN-10: 0-8006-3787-9 (alk. paper)
  1. Bible—Hermeneutics. 2. Postmodernism—Religious
aspects—Christianity. I. Title.
 BS476.A319 2006
 220.6'01—dc22
                                    2006011136

The paper used in this publication meets the minimum require-
ments of American National Standard for Information Sciences—
Permanence of Paper for Printed Library Materials, ANSI
Z329.48-1984.

Manufactured in the U.S.A.

10   09   08   07   06   1   2   3   4   5   6   7   8   9   10

CONTENTS

ACKNOWLEDGMENTS

Over the years I've worked through the ideas I describe here, I've benefited from the help of many, many friends, colleagues, assistants, and institutions—more indeed than I'll be able to catalog properly. I wrote some of these essays while on sabbatical leaves from Princeton Theological Seminary and Seabury-Western Theological Seminary. These leaves provided vital time for reflection and research, and I thank the deans and trustees of these schools for their support. My seminaries have likewise arranged for teaching, research, and administrative assistance. Among the many wonderful students who have helped me in this capacity, I especially thank my most recent Seabury assistants, Jane Schmoetzer and Elizabeth Scriven. Jane and Beth gracefully brought energy and order to an office that is (apart from their intervention) too often chaotic. I offer them warm thanks for their friendship and the generous persistence with which they hauled my abstracted teaching ministry back down to earth. My thanks to Richard Hays for his helpful comments throughout my elaboration of this project, and to Stanley Fish for emphatically (if not always successfully) correcting my misunderstandings concerning his work.

Beth Scriven also helped prepare the first draft of the book's manuscript, tracking down references and proposing translations of German sources (though I take responsibility for the final translations). Margaret Adam collaborated in that task and prepared the index. She then painstakingly examined the proofs, correcting as many of its faults as I would allow her to. Neil Elliott likewise has exercised a scholar's rigor, an editor's judicious attention to detail, and a valued friend's sympathetic patience.

Above all, though, I must thank the community of beloved friends and family whose advice, correction, wisdom, perspective, patience, humor, and steadfast convictions helped me fend off my most ludicrous errors, and who probably implanted all the best ideas I record here. Nothing could adequately express my affection and gratitude for their presence in my life, but this paltry note may signal what words fail to attain before they falter. I dedicate this book to summer days, long walks, late nights, and truth with David Cunningham; Emily and Monica Hittner-Cunningham; Teresa Hittner; Steve, Melinda, Liam, and Brendan Fowl; Kim, Katherine, Sarah Ann, Andrew, Peter, and Phil Kenneson and Chassy Freeman; Juliet Richardson; Jennifer Heckart; and Nathaniel, Josiah, Philippa, and Margaret Adam. Writing this morning from the intensity of Holy Week, I look forward to a glorious Easter with them, inseparable in spirit though we be scattered by mere geographic inconvenience. Thanks be to God for such rare and precious gifts!

Maundy Thursday 2006

Credits

Chapter 1: "Biblical Theology and the Problem of Modernity: Von Wredestrasse zu Sackgasse," *Horizons in Biblical Theology* 12 (1990): 1–18.

Chapter 2: "Docetism, Käsemann, and Christology: Why Historical Criticism Can't Protect Christological Orthodoxy," *Scottish Journal of Theology* 49:4 (1996): 391–410.

Chapter 3: "Twisting to Destruction: A Memorandum on the Ethics of Interpretation," *Perspectives in Religious Studies* 23 (1996): 215–22. An earlier form of this essay was presented to the Semiotics and Exegesis Section of the Society of Biblical Literature in November 1998. This essay owes much to Stephen Fowl, the SBL Semiotics and Exegesis Section, an Eckerd College class on New Testament ethics, and most recently the Critical Theology Group, especially Phil Kenneson, for refinements and criticisms of the memorandum in progress.

Chapter 4: "Matthew's Readers, Power, and Ideology," in *SBL 1994 Seminar Papers*, ed. Kent H. Richards (Atlanta: Scholars Press, 1994): 435–49.

Chapter 5: "Integral and Differential Hermeneutics," in *The Meanings We Choose*, ed. Charles Cosgrove (New York and London: T&T Clark, 2004): 24–38. This chapter owes much to conversations with principals in the discussion on which it reports, especially Stephen Fowl, Francis Watson, and Kevin Vanhoozer. As the original article took shape, Thomas Matrullo, Philip Cubeta, David Weinberger, Trevor Bechtel, and Margaret Adam teased, probed, challenged, encouraged, and refined the ideas that I propose, and I heartily thank them all.

Chapter 6: "Walk This Way: Repetition, Difference, and the Imitation of Christ," *Interpretation* 55:1 (2001): 19–33.

Chapter 7: "The Sign of Jonah: Getting the Big Picture (from a Fish-Eye View)," *Semeia* 51 (1990): 177–91.

Chapter 8: "Disciples Together, Constantly," in *Homosexuality and Christian Community*, ed. Choon Leong Seow (Louisville: Westminster John Knox, 1996): 123–32. I must convey my thanks to Juliet Richardson and to Philip Kenneson for their helpful criticisms of an earlier draft of this paper. I consider it a privilege to present this essay as a partial sign of my gratitude to my lesbian and gay sisters and brothers, who have taught me much about constancy, patient endurance, following a path of self-giving love, and the costs of truth.

Epilogue: "'He Placed Himself in the Order of Signs': Exegesis Signifying Theology" (paper presented to Christian Theology and the Bible Section, Society of Biblical Literature, Philadelphia, November 2005).

Introduction

Throughout the twentieth century, biblical scholars have grappled with the hermeneutical problem of how to connect their technical study of the grammar and historical context of the Bible with the ways the Bible can and should affect the lives of contemporary readers. They have suggested numerous work-arounds and improvements for hermeneutical deliberation, but none seems to have won general assent. Some people sense no problem with the status quo; they're content to puzzle over unusual verb forms, odd usages of familiar words, and the likelihood or unlikelihood of people raising other people from death. Yet a considerable number of readers express dissatisfaction with an interpretive method that excels at retrospect but falters when interpreters try to bring the Bible to bear on contemporary life.

In this book, I propose that readers who want something more than, or different from, the results of conventional critical scholarship may need to rethink some deeply held presuppositions of twentieth-century biblical hermeneutics. The historical-critical method—which I will hereafter also refer to as "technical biblical interpretation," to avoid reinforcing the impression that this array of interpretive moves constitutes a method—serves admirably, but it does not exhaust the work of interpretive reflection, nor does it set the terms on which further reflection must proceed. Indeed, many of the frustrations that students and clergy report involve expecting historical-critical reflection to provide sustenance that this mode of reading does not provide.

When scholars invoke the dominant mode of biblical interpretation as the definitive basis for theological readings of Scripture, it miscarries, for several reasons. The interpretive process breaks down because practitioners of this sort of scholarship rely on premises that have attained the status of axioms *within* the discipline, but when examined from a less narrow perspective, these conventions and axioms can no longer sustain the sense that they're self-evidently true. For instance, many scholars adhere to the myth of subsistent meaning, the premise that "meaning" is a characteristic quality inherent in a text. An exegete's job, then, requires him or her to distill that meaning from its raw form in the text to a purer, more manifest form.

As a second example, scholars who subscribe to the myth of subsistent meaning often locate responsibility for interpretive conclusions in the text itself, claiming that "the text requires this" or "the text permits that but not the other." Figures of speech that ascribe activity to the (inert) text work admirably when deployed as figures, but when they take on the character of literal ascriptions of agency to inert words, they disfigure our understanding of whence meaning comes and of who stands accountable for interpretive claims.

Third, contemporary interpreters tend to treat all interpretive deliberation as a more or less close approximation of verbal communication (hence, we speak of "body language" and suggest that "his expression spoke volumes"). Verbal communication, however, is a very peculiar example of communicative behavior. When we permit our experience with words to set the ground rules of interpretation, we conform the prevalent ordinary instances of communication to the extraordinary, highly regularized pattern of linguistic speech.

Fourth, as interpreters take the relatively more precise instance of verbal communication as the paradigm of communication in general, they tend to argue as though one and only one interpretation rightly ascertains the final (subsistent) meaning that the text expresses. The norm of monovalence pits interpreter against interpreter in a hermeneutical contest: only one, after all, can be right.

Finally, the adherents of current interpretive conventions warn that the alternative to conventional hermeneutical assumptions is interpretive chaos. The axioms I've described here lie at the foundation of contemporary hermeneutics. If, however, we allow that no lode of meaning lies embedded in our texts, that we (and not texts) sponsor and permit interpretations, that communication and interpretation constitute phenomena of far greater intricacy than the verbal paradigm allows, and that we may honestly and fairly consider the possibility that a given expression may mean several different things—if we yield on these points, the guild of biblical scholars suspects that we will disrupt the exquisite architecture of human communication (and especially, of course, of God's communication with humanity), rapidly declining into inarticulate grunts and brutality. To the contrary, though: interpreters who aim to tell the truth about God and humanity cannot afford to adhere to misleading premises about their interpretive work.

To the first, then: The widely held myth of subsistent meaning treats "meaning" as an immanent property of a text. A text has meaning as a quality independent of particular readers and particular circumstances. This premise arises from the amply justified intuition that when we express ourselves, we generally do so with the goal of evoking a particular sort of response, and we frequently succeed. We infer from this intuition that our successful expressions thus possess a particular quality that our interlocutors recognize, and that their assent demonstrates the soundness of that presence. In its sophisticated forms, the myth of subsistent meaning reasons that the intentional meaning of a textual expression—though not available to immediate perception—must be inferred from the ordered characteristics of that expression. The more striking the apparent evidence of harmony in expression and uptake, the more convincing the case for subsistent meaning. So when we admire the brilliance with which Daniel Defoe depicts the barbarity of religious intolerance in the anonymously published "The Shortest-Way with the Dissenters," we invest more confidently in the notion that there is some satiric meaning-quality with which Defoe imbued those particular words arranged in that order, and which we accurately discern when we recoil in horror at the prospect of hanging nonconforming preachers (speaking here as a general rule—each of us may preserve a little list of exceptions).

With so much to be said on behalf of subsistent meaning, how do I presume to question its existence? Simply on the basis that it isn't *there*, and that the apparent evidence of its existence derives more from the perceived necessity that it be there than from demonstration that it indeed subsists. The proponent of subsistent meaning demands (justly) that I account for correctness and incorrectness in communication if there be no independent touchstone for testing various proposed interpretations, and that I explain the demonstrable success of conversational interaction. The purchasers of this work, after all, located it on a bookshelf or in a catalog or database on the basis of verbal interactions. Yet subsistent meaning doesn't constitute a necessary ingredient to explain these phenomena. As I argue in the fourth chapter of this book, "The Shortest-Way" itself uses no obvious textual signals to indicate that Defoe meant the text to be construed as parody; indeed, it closely approximates the language that his Anglican adversaries themselves used against dissenters, and a good number of those High Churchmen approved of the measures that the tract proposed—until they found out that Defoe, himself a dissenter, wrote it. The apparent satiric meaning of "The Shortest-Way" derives not from the text of the tract, nor from the name Daniel Defoe that was eventually associated with the text, but from the complex of interactions and expectations from which we reckon that the dissenting author of the text, known to be a subtle and provocative writer, would not compose this essay against his own interest, but was using this pamphlet to highlight the barbarity of the High Churchmen's intolerance. Defoe might, after all, have had an abrupt conversion experience on the road to Newgate, or the essay might be misattributed. The axiom that meaning subsists in a text does not avail to explain the correct interpretation of "The Shortest-Way." Instead, we agree to regard that pamphlet as satire on the basis of unstated shared assumptions about how people behave, what we expect them to say under particular circumstances, how consistent we expect them to be, and so on—but not on the basis of a mystical intrinsic quality of "meaning" that some readers overlook and others recognize.

The same principle applies to more conventional communication: we infer meanings on the basis of a tremendous range of expectations and assumptions, tested and confirmed on the basis of frequent repetition and experimentation, but nonetheless only conventional and provisional. As demonstrated by failures of communication (lapses that occur much more routinely than overconfident models of subsistent meaning would allow), our expectations and conventions fail us regularly. Indeed, most of us in long-term intimate relationships must confess that even the highest degree of communicative familiarity with another person does not provide a sure basis for inferring meaning from their expressions. If meaning truly subsists in texts as a quality of the expression itself, why does it remain so elusive even under the conditions most favorable to mutual understanding, and how much more elusive must we admit that meaning to be in the expressions of people whom we know hardly at all?

If meaning does not subsist in texts, we must arrive at it some other way. On the approach that I propose here, we infer meaning from the experience of attempting to arrive at a shared understanding. Where communication proceeds smoothly, to mutual satisfaction, we sense that we apprehended what our interlocutor meant. Where communication breaks down, where one or more participants in a conversation seem not even to be disagreeing, we sense that someone doesn't understand what the other meant. "Meaning" helps us communicate by standing for the degree to which we believe ourselves to recognize what our interlocutor wishes us to understand (or vice versa). The advantage of this account of meaning lies in its capacity to shift attention from hidden properties of a text toward our role in proposing, approving, and evoking agreement over meaning. Suppose I want my neighbor to mow her lawn, so I tell her, "The grass is getting very long." She can justifiably suppose that I'm simply commenting on the remarkable vitality of her newly planted Kentucky Blue. If she construes my remark as a compliment, I need to try again, perhaps by saying, "It's about time to mow that lawn." This more direct entreaty will not guarantee that she apprehends my wishes, but most of the people with whom I've communicated would find the second invocation clearer than the first. We can criticize somebody who thinks the first statement should suffice to inspire immediate lawn mowing and commend the second statement as a laudably explicit request. We can sympathize with the neighbor who doesn't take up the subtle hint and deprecate the neighbor for whom the second doesn't provide adequate stimulus for home maintenance. Moreover, in all these cases, we can assess the question of meaning as cases of more or less plausible reasoning. We can ask interpreters to give an account of why one should infer such and such a meaning, and we can ask those who wish their expressions to evoke particular interpretations (rather than others) to express themselves in ways that provide reasons for deeming the desired interpretation most plausible. Instead of treating the text as a peculiar sort of silent agent that permits some interpretations and advocates, conceals, promotes, or resists others, this model keeps our attention squarely on humans who interpret one way rather than another, and on the reasons they advance for those interpretations.

As suggested by several passages in the preceding paragraphs, however, we communicate not solely with words, nor do we infer meaning only from linguistic signs. We have attained such proficiency in arriving at shared interpretation of our environment that we have a hard time recognizing that as a hermeneutical achievement. Nonetheless, the interpretive decisions by which we navigate our automobiles along crowded highways, the subtleties of facial aspect that alert us to shifts in our friends' moods, the environmental features that prompt us to take an umbrella to work—all these and infinitely many more instances of interpretation call on our capacity to draw interpretive conclusions from nonverbal data. Though these instances of interpretation elude our conscious attention, that does not make them less interpretive, and the staggering omnipresence of nonverbal interpretive apprehension should chasten our temptation to treat words as the preeminent example of occasions for interpretation.

The range of our nonverbal interpretation should teach us several vital lessons about biblical hermeneutics. Just as we would not suggest that a thundercloud, a tear on a cheek, or a rolling automobile's sudden swerve admits of one and only one correct interpretation, we should hesitate before we accept the axiom that verbal expressions have a single correct interpretation. Especially if we dispel the myth of subsistent meaning, we have only faint basis for supposing that the field of verbal communication uniquely requires a univocal interpretation. Indeed, even the domain of verbal expression inevitably involves dimensions of nonverbal communication. We appropriately sense that the monosyllable *HELP* scrawled in blood at the scene of some gruesome act of violence means something different from the comforting menu item at the top of my computer window. The simple word is the same in both cases, but the circumstantial cues—the shapes of the letters, the medium through which they're depicted, the rest of the visual field, for just a few—oblige our interpretive conscience to treat the two expressions very differently.

The qualities that inflect linguistic communication range from such prominent features as type design and page layout to the less obvious—for instance, the scent of the communication medium (a musty book, a perfumed letter, the ionized olfactory neutrality of a computer screen). Clement of Alexandria points to this aspect of hermeneutics when he complains that some heretical interpreters distort the appropriate sense of a biblical text by their intonation or inflection: "These are the people who, when they read, twist the Scriptures by their tone of voice to serve their own pleasures. They alter some of the accents and punctuation marks in order to force wise and constructive precept to support their taste for luxury" (*Stromateis* 3.29.2).[1] We can reverse the apparent sense of a sentence by sneering as we recite it, or render a vivid narrative painfully tedious by reading it without variation in tone.

An illuminating example of this phenomenon comes from the short-lived *Rutland Weekend Television* program produced by Eric Idle and Neil Innes after the demise of the *Monty Python's Flying Circus* program, a sketch fittingly entitled "Gibberish."[2] The sketch involves actors Eric Idle and Henry Woolf conversing as talk-show host and guest. Although they use perfectly intelligible words interspersed with conventional phrases ("Good evening and welcome," "I see," "drawn two, lost three"), their repartee makes no sense: "Rapidly piddlepot strumming Hanover peace pudding mouse rumpling cuddly corridor cabinets?" The actors deliver their lines, however, with the comfortable intonation of typical interview dialogue; the nonlinguistic aspects of the dialogue betray no indication that the words make no sense at all. Contrariwise, the participants in this interaction convey the impression that the short conversation satisfies them both: "Circular cup?" "*Circular cup!*" A listener cannot derive any coherent account of the linguistic exchange, but the general tenor of the dialogue comes across very clearly to anyone who has heard more than one or two broadcast talk shows. If intonation, emphasis, and delivery convey so much with a nonsensical script, they inevitably affect the interpretation of even marginally intelligible examples of verbal discourse.

This interplay of linguistic and nonlinguistic information in interpretation comes into focus in Julia Kristeva's distinction of *phenotext* and *genotext*, which I take up explicitly in the epilogue. Kristeva identifies a given expression's rule-governed, semantically and syntactically predictable structure as its phenotext. (Most biblical hermeneutics concentrates exclusively on phenotextual elements of the expressions we read from the Bible.) We never encounter a pure phenotext, however; every linguistic expression comes to us by way of particular circumstantial features. Printed texts involve elements of visual design; auditory texts involve articulation, volume, and tone. These aspects of the text, for which we can give no grammatical or lexical account, constitute the genotext. One can, of course, concentrate solely on one of these interpretive axes, but in so doing, one clamps a limit on the range of one's possible interpretations. By bringing genotextual considerations into play, theologically inclined interpreters can extend the scope of their interpretive exercises beyond the (phenotextual) boundaries that constrain them.[3] Sound interpretation involves questions of how one ought to portray, intone, and embody a text, as well as how the verbs should be parsed and what each word's semantic range covers.

At this point in my argument, I need hardly submit that the practice of interpretation affords innumerable reasons to expect that reasonable, learned, critical interpreters will develop different interpretations of the same biblical passage. Their disagreements need not imply that one alone has attained a true understanding of the text, whereas all others (now and before) have succumbed to the baneful effects of ignorance, dull wit, cultural accommodation, or perverse will. With a sensible degree of historical perspective, we will observe that the Bible has never known a period of unanimity in interpretation, nor has more than a century of rigorous technical scholarship ushered in an era of stable, scientifically certain interpretation. The history of

interpretations past and the prospects for interpretations to
come together give abundant evidence for the conclusion
that interpreters will always arrive at well-founded interpretations that diverge in irreconcilable ways.

While the range of *possible* interpretations is limitless,
the range of *plausible* interpretations extends much less far. A
solipsistic interpreter can always make an outlandish suggestion about who the two witnesses of Revelation 11:3 might
be, but unless he or she can advance reasons to assent to that
proposition—for instance, the idea that the two witnesses
were John Reeve and his cousin Lodowick Muggleton[4]—
that proposal remains an idiosyncrasy. To the extent that we
can elicit reasons for particular interpretations and measure
them against criteria we can identify and articulate, interpretive difference need not be accounted a weakness. As James
K. A. Smith has suggested, the plenitude of interpretations
may more cogently reflect God's abundant generosity given
in creation than testify to the confusion of tongues imposed
on humanity at Babel.[5]

On the basis of the preceding paragraphs, then, I submit that the risk of Western civilization and the Christian
faith collapsing, undermined by the pernicious influence of
a hermeneutics of difference, has been greatly exaggerated.
For all the bluster about single, univocal, uniquely correct
meanings that allegedly subsist in texts, churches (and civilization) have had to get along with the demonstrable daily
fact of interpretive difference. Rival critics have worked out
their differences by arguing over the best reasons to adopt
one rather than another, and abundant alternative readings
seem to flourish all the more in this rigorously technical
interpretive environment. If the church and the West are
tottering on the brink of catastrophe, it would be hard to
make a case that a positive approach to interpretive difference explains its condition.

In fact, by acknowledging the points that I have sketched
thus far, interpreters with theological interests in the Bible
stand to benefit immensely. Freed from the impossible task

of pinning down a single correct meaning for each biblical passage, scholars might devote their efforts to spelling out what makes their proposal the best among various legitimate hypotheses. Interpreters who adopt this position would make themselves accountable for defining the specific contexts and criteria by which they legitimate their readings, rather than pretending to make a case that should convince every single competent reader.

Even more positively, interpreters who attend from the outset to the multivocal, nonlinguistic dimensions of communication benefit from the opportunity to venture readings that do not fit squarely into the competitive and exclusive ethos of biblical studies. An Anglican's theological interpretation of Scripture will thus appropriately differ from an Independent Baptist's; neither will need to try to prove that Jesus, had he the opportunity, would surely have belonged to one or the other denomination. Above all, a hermeneutics that acknowledges the significance of gesture, intonation, image, flavor, and tactile perception incorporates at the outset the pertinence of the interpreter's enacted, articulated, depicted, savored interpretive endeavors. No iron curtain separates this mode of biblical interpretation from ethics, from doctrinal reflection, from liturgy and pastoral care, and these considerations enter into critical interpretive analysis not as an afterthought but as a positive integral element of the hermeneutical process.

The chapters of this book approach this multimodal differential hermeneutics with various points of emphasis, along various trajectories. Each chapter sets out to clarify a particular puzzle relevant to understanding the transition away from modern technical interpretation to a hermeneutic that better fits a more interactive, flexible approach to meaning. Written over the course of fifteen years, the chapters of this book begin from a critical interrogation of what was once the prevalent theoretical background for New Testament theology and gradually stake out a staging area for articulating a sounder approach to the theological interpretation of the Bible.

The first chapter considers the relation between modern biblical scholarship and the goal of a satisfying theological interpretation of Scripture. Many readers of the Bible report a certain disorientation when they turn to the study of biblical theology. They may have learned well the academic modes of criticism that form the basis of contemporary biblical interpretation, and they may feel a strong interest in how the Bible informs subsequent theological reflection, but the most prominent texts in biblical theology offer something very different from the wisdom these readers seek. A reader who turns to a biblical theology book in hope of learning the biblical precedents for Trinitarian formulas is more likely to encounter a historical survey of the discipline of biblical theology itself, and programmatic reflections on how biblical theology should be done. Often as not, both the history and the program baffle the reader. So the interested reader's hermeneutical vigor dissipates in thickets of dense disciplinary undergrowth. The miscarriage of one program leads to proposals for another, and this new alternative requires historical perspective in order to justify its claims, and in turn baffles a new set of readers.

Chapter 1 proposes that the definitions by which biblical theology and New Testament theology establish their disciplinary identity include elements that correspond to the axiomatic assumptions of modern culture. In particular, the practitioners in these fields have so defined their disciplines as to put a premium on the presumed "scientific" character of the knowledge they produce. They show a proclivity for according greater weight to the most recent studies of their topics, in keeping with the modern ideology of progress (as though sound understanding of the New Testament had only dawned in the most recent decade). Accordingly, New Testament theologians emphasize the vast historical gap between the ancient New Testament context and the contemporary scene, a gap that requires the mediating expertise of a historical scholar; from this point of view, the generations of interpreters between Paul and this morning constitute more of an obstacle to understanding the Scriptures than they provide links to a living tradition of interpretation. The modern theological interpreter rejects these readers of Scripture as "precritical," since they do not conform to the same criteria that the modern scholar regards as necessary. Modern biblical theology withholds its approval from any mode of interpretation that does not submit to adjudication at the bar of historical scholarship. However, this chapter holds open the possibility that biblical theology may have durable claims to legitimacy that do not depend on strictly modern assumptions about time, progress, and the unique validity of historical-critical analysis. The strongest ventures in biblical theology demonstrate insight and critical judgment that draw on historical-critical scholarship but cannot be limited to the horizons that circumscribe modern technical conventions of reading.[6]

The second chapter confronts one of the most common rationales for assigning historical-critical analysis the authority to adjudicate questions of interpretive legitimacy. The historian, it is argued, brings to light the historical actuality of Jesus' identity, so any other approach to studying Jesus displaces his fully human character in favor of a theological phantasm (the christological error of "Docetism"). This defense of historical-critical authority, however, misconstrues the results of technical historical scholarship and misreads the (historical) character of Docetism. Careful study of the topic of Docetism in its patristic context and in its contemporary manifestations reveals an elusive complex of tendencies and inclinations, no one of which can be remedied by historical scholarship. Nor indeed can technical scholarship produce an anti-docetic, concretely human Jesus on its own; historical research into Jesus produces an academic construct (as opposed, perhaps, to a devotional construct), but the academic construct does not automatically count as more fully incarnate than its devotional alternative. The opposite of Docetism is not certified historical scholarship, but a resolutely Chalcedonian Christology.

The third chapter takes up the problem of subsistent meaning and textual agency. If, as I argue, texts do not possess characteristics that promote or resist various interpretations, can one simply make a text mean anything one chooses? By no means! Our interactions with texts and the interpretations we offer always involve social and environmental mediation. Communities of interpreters approve or discountenance proposed interpretations according to criteria that constitute the community: technical interpreters according to criteria of academic scholarship, congregations of faithful believers according to the rule of their faith, and enthusiastic consumers of sensation according to the headlines of supermarket tabloids. Mortal readers have no access to immutable laws of interpretation by which we can, with God's perspective on meaning, adjudicate interpretive legitimacy, but we cannot escape participation in complex interactions that provide ample basis for evaluating interpretations. We can "make texts mean whatever we want" only if we are willing to abide the consequences of alienating everyone who deems our readings nonsensical. When we emphasize our own accountability for the interpretations we propose (rather than invoking transcendent laws of interpretation whose application always remains contested in particular cases), we open up a strong connection between our hermeneutics and the ethics we proclaim and practice.

The fourth chapter pursues the question of meaning and ethics with particular reference to the Gospel of Matthew's invective against Jesus' rivals and enemies. While critics have denounced Matthew as "anti-Jewish," this chapter argues that an ethically sound reading (in the sense set out in chapter three) should promote a different view of Matthew and his theology. There is not, in other words, an anti-Jewish meaning subsisting in Matthew's Gospel. Our readings of Matthew have benign or baneful effects on our neighbors, Gentile and Jewish, but it's up to us to articulate interpretations for which we are willing to stand accountable. After all, Matthew's Gospel quotes many harsh words Jesus directed against Gentiles and instructs disciples to uphold the entire Torah; if Matthew himself was Jewish and deplored rival visions of how Judaism should be constituted, his polemics should be treated as "anti-Pharisaism" or as intra-Judaic controversy, rather than as anti-Judaism. Finally, I appeal to the historical experience of the great crisis of the mid-twentieth century to show that the ideologues of Nazi anti-Semitism specifically rejected the Gospel of Matthew as unsuitable for their propaganda purposes, whereas some of the Protestants who risked their lives to save Jewish refugees acted on the distinctively Matthean basis that whoever offers aid or shelter to one of the least of Jesus' sisters and brothers does so to Jesus. While Christians have certainly drawn on Matthean texts to justify their anti-Jewish bigotry, we should not blame Matthew for that bigotry. Instead, we should hold interpreters accountable for the use they make of texts, and we should exemplify the kind of commitment to support and protect our neighbors that would make anti-Jewish readings of Matthew seem implausible.

Chapter 5 returns to the theoretical dimension of theological hermeneutics, discussing the relative benefits and drawbacks of approaches to interpretation that foreground either univocality and correctness, or multiple meanings and soundness. The first approach, which I label "integral hermeneutics," coheres admirably with God's unity and with hermeneutical analysis that seeks the definite meaning of a particular expression. Integral hermeneutics often upholds the premise that meaning subsists in texts, and it issues the ethical mandate that interpreters orient their readings toward the author's intended meaning. The alternative perspective locates meaning not within texts, but in the manifold interactions of humans with texts or of humans with other humans. In this complex economy of interpretation, we nonetheless find many of the most careful, diligent, faithful, and learned readers reaching divergent conclusions about what a given text means. Rather than taking this as evidence that only one of them is right and the rest more or less mistaken, the second approach to interpretation takes this as a reason to regard difference in interpretation as a normative condition; hence, I label this approach "differential hermeneutics." The strength of differential hermeneutics lies in its capacity to ascribe disagreement to causes other than error or ignorance. On this account, we can expect interpreters often to disagree with one another, even as we expect the best interpretations to adduce carefully reasoned cases to justify their conclusions. While both approaches to interpretation can advance cogent reasons why their perspective offers value to theological interpreters, the practice of differential hermeneutics attenuates the spirit of contentiousness, better befits the capacities and limitations of mortal interpreters, and admits a fuller range of interpretive expression than does an integral hermeneutics. To this extent at least, a differential hermeneutics affords the prospect of a more harmonious practice of biblical interpretation, attentive to the myriad particularities that constitute biblical interpreters as different people, with a view toward embodying the truths we claim to learn from the Bible.

The sixth chapter considers the importance of living out one's interpretation of the Bible with special attention to the complications attendant on the imitation of Christ. Critics have noted an array of weaknesses of imitation-ethics: they allege that "imitation" disrupts the proper roles of the Savior and the saved, tends to reduce the gospel's daunting imperious command to the banalities of polite good citizenship, and imposes a hegemony of the homogeneous. Still, a number of warrants bolster the case on behalf of the imitation of Christ. Most obviously, Scripture seems to mandate this way of earnest discipleship, and consequently we can sensibly expect that the lives of Christians bear at least a vague resemblance to the life of Jesus. We can maintain the value of an ethic of imitation if we attend to differences as well as similarities, if we distinguish the imitation of Christ from the misguided effort to become our own messiahs. By respecting the constitutive role that difference plays in repetition and identity, we can affirm solidarity without requiring assimilation, ordering our differences to foster harmonious community rather than stifling monotony. Thus, we can sponsor an imitation of Christ's unwavering faithfulness to the gospel that respects distinctions and particularities at the same time it draws us ever closer to one another and to God.

Chapter 7 tests the claims of modern integral hermeneutics against the evidence of actual interpretive practice. If we must accede to the premise that a single subsistent meaning lurks within texts, we may reasonably ask that two thousand years of scrupulously close study bring that meaning into finer focus. As a sample, I introduce the saying from the Gospels wherein Jesus alludes to the sign of Jonah. This saying intrigued the church's early commentators, among whom it evoked a remarkably diverse array of interpretations. If, as some scholars of hermeneutics suggest, we can ascribe this to the undisciplined imaginations of archaic spiritual interpretation, we ought to see a significant convergence among interpreters with the advent of critical technical scholarship. In fact, though, the interpretations of twentieth-century scholars give no clear indication that their shared commitment to scientific investigative method has brought them closer to consensus. Although one can always criticize interpretations relative to premises that particular bodies of readers uphold, no one set of interpretive presuppositions itself provides a key to unlocking textual puzzles.

Chapter 8 approaches the problem of ways one can articulate a richly biblical theology of human sexuality and hallowed relationships. In an effort to move beyond an impasse in which opposing parties cling to a handful of texts, this chapter seeks evidence for a general understanding of God's will for human intimacy, from which to work out a theological explanation of what makes particular expressions of sexual intimacy commendable or condemnable. By reading Scripture's accounts of the character and implications of holy intimacy, particularly as the prophets and apostles apply it to God's relationship with humanity, this chapter develops criteria for discerning what characteristics bespeak holiness in intimacy and how churches may face the difficult challenge of putting that discernment into practice.

Finally, the epilogue introduces the concept of signifying practices, drawn from cultural criticism, as a heuristic device for understanding the relation of disciplined technical interpretation to theological, ethical, liturgical, and pastoral practice. When we bring critical attention to the full range of communicative action, we cannot justify restricting interpretive legitimacy to the phenotextual dimensions of textual expression, nor can we limit in advance the range of interpretive gestures. This essay draws the conceptual vocabulary of signifying practices into the interaction among the different related areas of theological interest, asking how the lives we make constitute an enacted exegesis of the gospel. As the eternal Word entered the temporal economy of signification in order to make God known, so exegetical theologians can use their critical faculties not only to fine-tune our appreciation of verb tenses, allusions, and scribal tendencies, but all the more to encourage the people of God more persistently, more wisely, more persuasively to make visible the truth toward which our interpretive labors aim.

With the epilogue on signifying practices, this series of forays into unfamiliar terrain closes. What I offer here amounts only to the report of an exploratory expedition; much remains to be done, from surveying and planning to assessing the various ways by which one might dwell in this habitat. In the end, what I pass along turns out to involve less a discovery of something new than a critical reappropriation of ways that faithful readers have interpreted Scripture and sought to direct their hearts and souls and minds and strength toward loving God more truly. That effort always begins, never ends, and only benefits from sharing the vocation of discipleship.

CHAPTER ONE

Biblical Theology and the Problem of Modernity

In recent years, biblical theology has been pronounced moribund, declared to be in crisis, and generally found wanting. The evident problem is not so much that no one wants to *do* biblical theology as that no one seems capable of living up to the demands of those who theorize about biblical theology. Proposed theologies are too harmonistic, too diffuse, too apologetic, or too uncritical. Apparently nothing is left to do but debate what biblical theology should be, if only we could have some. Is biblical theology a near-dead horse, still subject to occasional floggings at the hands of hard-nosed historical critics and to futile attempts at resuscitation by theologically inclined scholars—or can these bones live?

The answer I propose is, "Yes, they can live. But first we must reexamine the nature of biblical theology's near-fatal afflictions." A careful consideration will show that quite probably, those who have been trying to get the old gray mare back on her feet again have been consulting the wrong veterinarian. I suggest that the travails of modern biblical theology come from the contradictions inherent in the effort to attain satisfactorily theological results while respecting modernity's rules. Anyone who desires different results will have to do what is, for *modern* biblical scholars, unthinkable: to abandon the effort to construct a biblical theology on a historical foundation.

What Is "Modern"?

In this context, "modernity" does not refer to the quality of being particularly recent, though the dominance of distinctly modern benchmarks for interpretation is a relatively recent phenomenon. Rather, modernity designates a specific interpretation of what is to be done in a given discipline; it is a label for a set of assumptions that underlies and regulates an enterprise. There are admittedly as many different kinds of modernity as there are people who think about modernity, and to that extent my thesis is too ambiguous.[1] The modernity to which I am pointing will not be found in self-conscious stylistic reflection on biblical studies. (Perhaps just to that extent, Joseph O'Leary is correct that we have not yet attained modernity.[2]) My quarry in this essay is a more dilute, less self-conscious, and therefore more pervasive *vulgarized* modernity.[3] It is the sort of modernity one might expect to find in a discipline that has never come to grips with the underpinnings of its own cultural situation, its own modernity.[4]

Lacking an authoritative definition of "modernity," I will stipulate the following characteristics: first, a proclivity for the adjective *scientific*; second, a pattern of citing newer sources as most authoritative; and third, a reluctance to admit that current biblical interpretations stand in continuity with biblical interpretation through the centuries. There is a fourth mark of modernity—namely, the assumption that any interpretation that does not exercise *historical* criticism is "uncritical" or "precritical," as though historical interpretation provides the only legitimate criteria for judgment— but this mark of biblical-critical modernity will be discussed later in this chapter.

Defenders of the scientific character of biblical interpretation generally rush to point out that, in the context of the humanities, the word *scientific* is standing in for the German *wissenschaftlich*. This word, it is alleged, carries less of the ideological freight associated with *scientific* in English. Yet if this were strictly true, and if English-speaking biblical scholars were concerned to distance themselves from the connotations of objectivity, precision, and lawlike universality that attach to claims of scientific status, they might easily opt to call their studies scholarly or learned. Clearly, however, in our cultural situation, the word *scientific* confers an aura of greater reliability. Consider, for example, how scholars in the humanities scrabble to justify associating their work with the sciences, and how few scholars in the sciences would be eager to classify their work with the humanities. *Modern* knowledge is scientific knowledge.[5] Modern knowledge is also based only on the most up-to-date scholarship. We presumably have little or nothing to learn from our scholarly forebears, except what we may learn from the mistakes they made. One need do no more than examine the footnotes in any issue of the *Journal of Biblical Literature* to see the frequency of references to works of the last twenty or thirty years, and the paucity of references to the nineteen centuries before that. This phenomenon is explained by underlining the vast advances that biblical studies have made, but those advances appear dramatic only against the backdrop of *modern* criteria.[6] In fact, we are not appreciably closer now to a consensus on the interpretation of any given text than we have ever been, particularly if the interpretations of "noncanonical" readers are taken into account.[7]

Modern scholars also advise us that we need to overcome a hermeneutical abyss that divides us from the biblical texts. This argument frequently is made with cavalier references to what modern people can or cannot believe. It would be convenient simply to accept this claim on its own terms, saying, "All right; the people who can't believe this we will call 'modern,' and those who can believe it are just not 'modern people,'" but in so doing we would conceal the extent to which even those who dispute "can't believe" claims usually do so within the bounds decreed by modern interpretation.[8]

For the purposes of this chapter, then, modernity refers to these criteria, which (implicitly and explicitly) have settled into a hegemonic rule over the academic discourse of biblical studies. Since the criteria of this modernity have generally been formed in the practice of interpretation and in its institutional channels of dissemination (accreditation, publication, and employment), they have tended to come to light only occasionally, as when Krister Stendahl proposed the now-familiar distinction between what the Bible *means* and what it *meant*.[9] More often, the assumptions of this modernity remain behind the scenes; to get them on stage, I will tell a story that may help us see behind the curtain to the backstage of modern biblical theology.

Modernism on Stage

The drama whose scenery we shall explore is a battle story. It begins offstage, before the opening curtain, in 1958, when Alan Richardson published *An Introduction to the Theology of the New Testament*.[10] The curtain opens six years later, with the publication of a review article in *Novum Testamentum*, written by Leander Keck.[11]

Keck's review is a minor landmark in the field of scholarly polemics. Whereas Richardson's greatest offense was incorporating a couple of lamentable opinions in his preface and footnotes, Keck responds with a twenty-page denunciation of every aspect of the book from the table of contents to the conclusion. (There are no condemnations of the index.) If Keck is to be believed, Richardson is guilty of enough interpretive crimes to send him up the theological river for a long stretch. As we review the plaintiff's case, I will extract from his arguments criteria of judgment that are typical of the sort of biblical-critical modernity I'm illustrating.

For a first example, Keck is distressed that Richardson admits having assumed that it is particularly appropriate to explain Christian origins from the point of view of Christian faith. "A portrait of the NT and its Church which does not [disturb] comforting convictions," he warns, "is itself suspect until it legitimizes itself" (220). On this account, good modern interpretations are impossible if the scholar does not set aside any prior commitment to the truth of the New Testament, and interpretations that aim to overturn the beliefs of orthodox or Catholic believers are ipso facto more credible than interpretations that suggest the New Testament authors (and those who trust them) were right after all.

A second complaint involves the arrangement of Richardson's book, which covers a variety of theological topics. Keck is concerned that "[this] procedure might by-pass precisely what is most characteristic of the NT mode of theologizing—the correlating of topics which are here rent asunder" (221).

Keck also finds Richardson insufficiently appreciative of the results of research in *Religionsgeschichte* (history of religions) and *Dogmengeschichte* (history of dogma). This is, he says, the book's "fatal flaw" (234).

Fourth, Keck doubts that Richardson is hermeneutically sophisticated enough to accomplish the task he has undertaken. Richardson does not, according to Keck, pay enough attention to the gap between what the New Testament meant and what it means today. According to Keck, "To most men [*sic*] biblical jargon sounds like jibberish" (240). Keck wants a theology that addresses the vast cultural difference between the first and twentieth centuries by constructing a historical model that both reflects the utterly alien worldview of the New Testament and mediates this unintelligible message in concepts we can understand.

To summarize: Christian faith is out of place in biblical theology. Biblical theology must proceed on the basis of rigorous methodological skepticism. Biblical theology is to be presented according to a historical plan that offers a separate hearing to each theological voice in the New Testament. Modern biblical theology must presume a stronger influence from Hellenistic or pagan sources than from Old Testament/Jewish sources. Finally, biblical theology must address and overcome the distinction between "what it meant" and "what it means today."

Keck did not promulgate these criteria alone. The leading biblical theologians of our time have held most or all of these principles as necessary, and in what we may fairly call the most influential recent article on the subject of biblical theology, Krister Stendahl has defined these as the ground rules by which the biblical theology game must be played.[12] While his essay is best remembered for codifying the distinction between "what it meant" and "what it means," Stendahl also calls attention to the importance of noncanonical material (428ff.), of treating individually the conflicting theological positions in the Bible (426 and passim), and of research in history of religions (418 and passim). Though Stendahl does not explicitly advise the adoption of methodological skepticism, which was one of Keck's presuppositions, he offers a fair clue to his feelings by ignoring conservative biblical theologians.

What is most important about these criteria is not their universality—that could be debated indefinitely—but the fact that these eminent scholars see them as self-evident. The preponderance of modern critics assume without hesitation that one cannot undertake a theological exposition of Scripture without first having satisfied a jury of dubious jetage scholars who have, at least for the time being, set aside their religious convictions. This assumption leads quite naturally to the other criteria. If there are differing historical situations relevant to the theologies of Genesis and Revelation, then these books must be treated separately in biblical theology. An analysis that assigns cardinal importance to the Old Testament roots of New Testament theology is, as Keck points out, under suspicion of too easily harmonizing the two and of neglecting the Hellenistic pagan contribution to the New Testament.[13] (One could make a similar argument against interpreting Old Testament myths apart from their ancient Semitic analogues.)

Questioning the Assumptions

All this follows naturally if the criteria are justified. But these criteria themselves present the would-be biblical theologian with a tremendous obstacle. What sort of biblical theology can we extract from the countless different voices that historical criticism has shown us in and behind the biblical texts? What is the meaning of the idea "biblical theology" if it is methodologically required to make extensive reference to *non*biblical material? If the cultural gap between then and now is as great as we are told, we are surely justified in wondering whether only the lightest and most fragile theological tenets can cross that abyss. We may wonder whether it is even worth bothering to try.

While I have underlined the extent to which modernity's program for biblical theology has become the assumed criterion, I have not yet given sufficient reason for changing course. Such an argument is hard to develop, since a criterion that can safely be assumed is rarely defended. Yet the canons by which modern interpreters judge biblical theology finally rely on historical criticism as a *necessary criterion* for theological interpretation.[14] My goal in this section of the chapter is to show how this necessity is something that modern biblical theology itself posits, rather than being a natural necessity.

THE DEFENSE

Those who defend the necessity of historical criticism can take one of three courses. First, they may point to the origins of biblical theology as a distinctive enterprise, to show that historical-critical investigation is integral to the discipline as it has been practiced from the beginning. Or they may argue that one simply can't correctly understand the biblical texts themselves without historical criticism. Third, they may argue that historical investigation is essential to Christian theology. Christian faith involves truth claims about what actually happened—and happens—in the world. All these arguments are utterly convincing to scholars who share modern presuppositions; thus, they appear to represent knock-down justification for the modern position. But for the same reason, they cannot seem convincing to a biblical theologian who does not share those presuppositions, as I will illustrate here.

The argument from the origins of biblical theology describes the discipline's emergence in the aftermath of Johann Philipp Gabler's inaugural address at Altdorf in 1787, "On the Proper Distinction between Biblical and Dogmatic Theology,"[15] in which he established the necessity of beginning biblical theology from a strictly historical foundation. Of course, modern scholars agree that Gabler missed the boat on one point: he wanted to derive timeless, unconditioned truths from the time-conditioned historical foundation he had laid. William Wrede developed what has become the standard modern reinterpretation of Gabler: since there is no timeless truth to be found, biblical theology is nothing but the enterprise of building a historical foundation and then stopping. That is why Wrede argued that *sogennanten* (so-called) New Testament theology should properly be called "the history of early Christian religion" (116).[16] Wrede's followers have resumed the quest for something more than history by seeking out a contingent (not timeless) contemporary theological translation of the ancient theologoumena that form the historical foundation Gabler sought.

This effort to do more than Wrede while at the same time maintaining the necessary historical perspective drives home what modern biblical theologians see as a self-evident truth: there is a gross discontinuity between what biblical texts meant in their original context and what they mean today. This distinction is canonized in Krister Stendahl's well-known article on biblical theology in the *Interpreter's Dictionary of the Bible*,[17] wherein he claims that the biblical theologian's task is *descriptive*, whereas the systematic theologian's task is *normative*. That is, a biblical theologian fulfills Wrede's project by telling us what the texts *meant*, while the systematic theologian promulgates theological norms built upon the biblical foundation her colleague has provided. We have seen this distinction earlier in this essay, when Keck assailed Richardson for failing to recognize this great ugly ditch.

Lying behind both of these arguments is the fundamental conviction that Christian (and/or Jewish) theology can't be divorced from historical reflection without losing something distinctively, perhaps essentially, Christian (or Jewish). The modern biblical theologian reasons that even if we don't know "how it actually was," we are obliged by the very character of our faith to seek out the historical truth about Jesus, the early community, and their texts—and then to restrict our theologizing to what can be inferred from that residuum. This assumption motivates the conservative modern critic's labors to prove the historicity of such historically improbable events as the virgin birth or the stilling of the storm. It likewise grounds the liberal modern critic's effort to figure out what, if anything, one can say about Jesus, and it is the basis of this assumption that there can be no one biblical theology, but rather an irreducible plurality of biblical theologies.

Not So Obvious

The modern interpreter sees these three arguments on the one hand as obvious, and on the other as utterly devastating critiques of any opposing position. But their force resides principally in their having been inculcated into generations of biblical scholars. If one examines them apart from the prior assumption that history has anything important to do with biblical theology, these knock-down arguments look rather feeble.

The alleged source for modern biblical theology—Gabler's lecture—can just as well be read in a way that undercuts the assumption that the history of the discipline justifies reliance on history.[18] Ben Ollenburger points out that Gabler adopted the criterion of history because he thought it provided "the only reliable criterion for determining what is . . . dispensable."[19] He wanted to establish what was merely historical in order to be rid of it, leaving only "the unchanging testament of Christian doctrine."[20] He would no doubt have been startled by the way in which modern interpreters have scuttled to retrieve the husk he was eager to throw away. It would be misleading, then, to depict the biblical-theological quest simply as a search for the historical truths about early Christianity. Indeed, the history of modern biblical theology could more fairly be narrated as the tale of earnest scholars trying to reach the North Pole by traveling west. Biblical theologians readily adopted Gabler's strategy. But since they have emphasized what Gabler thought was the inferior part of the project, they have been persistently frustrated in efforts to attain the superior part.

The second proposed basis for the necessity of historical verification for biblical theology—that is, the distinction between what the text meant and what it means—is no better founded. In the first place, it quite arbitrarily concentrates on discontinuity in interpretation, without even considering the fact that when a text has been interpreted every day for over nineteen centuries, there will be important continuity of interpretation. It is not as though we have come upon the biblical texts as relics from an utterly alien culture, with no connection whatever to our lives. The Bible is a foundational document of Western culture, to the extent that most acculturated people can quote from the Bible by memory (at least with a little prompting). Bible readers generally believe—mistakenly, if we are to trust modern interpreters[21]—that they understand almost all of what they read.

This continuity in interpretation also provides a defense against another claim for the importance of historical interpretation. It is sometimes claimed that historical research is necessary for understanding, since we rely on historical knowledge anyway; that is, we use historical knowledge in every aspect of interpreting the Bible, beginning from translation, so that we are obligated to continue this historical research indefinitely until we reach a satisfactory historical judgment. Whatever the merits of this argument in theory (and I have grave doubts about it), in practice it can be rephrased as, "If you don't agree with me, you need to do more historical homework." In fact, the continuity of interpretation transmitted indirectly through cultural influences and directly through homiletics and catechesis provides ample historical guidance for most Bible readers. The *quality* of that guidance may be disputed, but the claim that people have urgent need of help in crossing an immense cultural chasm is very different from the claim that some of the ample help they have is not just right, and it is the former claim that Krister Stendahl makes.

The means/meant distinction is problematic not only because it rests on one-sided assumptions about the discontinuity of interpretation, but also because it is not entirely clear that the distinction works. In a painstaking analysis of this distinction, Ollenburger shows that, on Stendahl's account, the interpreter, the text, time, and meaning interact in ways that are very peculiar (if not outright incoherent).[22] Among other problems, Stendahl would interpose three or four mediations between the systematician's version of meaning and the text in question (text → biblical theologian → original meaning → systematic theologian → contemporary meaning).

At the heart of Stendahl's proposal is the belief that historicality, in the sense of both "real historical accuracy" and "relativity to a given temporal situation," has attained the status of a cognitive given for modern interpreters. To count, any reality must be a real historical reality; and by virtue of its historical fixation, this reality is so remote for us that we must rely on highly credentialed specialists to reproduce for us the original circumstances of that reality. The failure to account for the mediation that diminishes (if it does not annihilate) the gap in question, and the convoluted relation of interpreter to text imposed by the posited "meaning gap," counts heavily against the distinction between "means" and "meant."

Historical criticism might never have attained its hegemonic grip on interpretive method if there were not a lurking conviction that there is a historical imperative to the Christian faith. More to the point, it is believed that as the scholarly understanding of "history" has changed, the theological interest in history is to have changed apace. This assumption is particularly dangerous when combined with the characteristic of contemporary biblical studies that may be called residual positivism—that is, the belief that the difference between *wie es eigentlich gewesen ist* (how it actually was) and our historical descriptions is real but not functional. "Of course, we can't know exactly what Isaiah was thinking, but we have to come as close as we can." When the demand that theology's interests in history correspond to a particular understanding of history, especially an understanding that has been developed quite apart from any theological interests, combines with a definition of history that encourages a quest for almost-but-not-quite-attainable historical facts, theology can be nothing other than a speculative metaphysical offshoot of the larger discipline of history, and theology will never be permitted to posit what must be contradicted by the results of historical research.

There is a final objection I have not yet even hinted at. It is the common fear that if we let go our death grip on historical verification, we will be conceding defeat to the fundamentalist (or relativist) hordes surrounding our bastion of free inquiry (or doctrinal purity). To the credit of this feeling, we all remember that historical criticism arose as a strategy of resistance against hegemonic theological discourses, and in some contexts it retains that quality to this day. This does not, however, justify the claim that historical criticism is necessary across the board. If we can find no better tactic for resisting a distasteful theological option, then we may as well admit that there is little difference between our position (maintaining the necessity of historical criticism) and theirs (execrating the practice). Fundamentalism will be thwarted not by doing more ardent historical work, but by seeking out a sounder construal of Christianity.

If this situation sounds familiar—somewhat like the situation of biblical theology in the contemporary academic scene—you will understand why I submit that we have to start fresh at the task of biblical theology. Modern biblical theology begins with a particular construal of the terms *theology* and *biblical*, and of their relation. Of course, this is not the only possible construal of biblical theology, but it is the one with which virtually all of us are so familiar that we feel uneasy and disoriented without it. The remainder of this chapter comprises an exercise in what I hope will be fruitful disorientation, to sketch what biblical theology might look like.

Contingent Criteria

In my effort to show that the criterion of historical verification is not necessary to biblical theology, but is contingent upon the interests of a particular cultural and academic tradition, I may have created two misleading impressions. The first is that one can make any sort of claim about biblical theology without having to justify the claim historically. Quite the contrary; if you want to make historical claims, as many theologians in our current cultural situation do, I will demand that you be prepared with historical arguments. I understand that others may need to account for historical scholarship in their theologies, but that does not necessitate advancing historical claims in every legitimate biblical theology.

The second possible misunderstanding would see my claim as entailing that, absent the necessity of a historical criterion, we are left altogether without criteria. This is the assumption that lies behind the gesture of labeling interpretations "precritical" or "uncritical" if they do not show due regard for historical-critical methods. But on what other basis can we judge which biblical theologies to commend, which to condemn? After all, I have just underlined the extent to which criteria are contingent upon the situation of the critic. The absence of *necessary* criteria, though, leaves a multitude of other *contingent* criteria for evaluating biblical theologies,[23] and it is to these that I will proceed.

BACK TO BASICS

First, the name *biblical theology*, if it is to be used without flagrant affront to the conventions of our discourse, justifies certain criteria. So—and I risk the accusation of belaboring the obvious because this point has been contested by modern biblical theologians—a biblical theology will have to do with theology, with theological topics and concerns. Not with the religion of Israel, not with the religion of the first Christians, but with theology as we know it and as we care about it, including topics such as creation, the Trinity, soteriology, ecclesiology, and so on, which are usually excluded from biblical theology on the ground that they reflect the theologian's interest rather than an interest inherent in the text. When a proposed biblical theology seems to have little to do with the discipline of theology, we should not (Wrede notwithstanding) assume that we were wrong about the name of the discipline. If I opened a book that purported to be a dictionary and found therein nothing but Mother Goose rhymes, I would not assume I had misunderstood what a dictionary is; I would decline to recognize the work in question as a dictionary and would look for another that provided the spelling, pronunciation, and definition of words.

Likewise, the theological content of the work should be handled in a way that is at least arguably "biblical." I don't believe we can define the modifier too closely at this stage of my argument. Suffice it to say that the text of the Bible should function as source, or warrant, or basis for the alleged biblical theology. There will be arguments over what is truly biblical, but that is fitting. "Biblical" here refers not just to having a long index of references to Scripture, but to the arena within which the argument is taking place.[24]

These two criteria don't seem very weighty, but they already rule out much of what has been published as biblical theology under the influence of modernity. Wrede, you will recall, thought that the name *New Testament theology* was wrong in both terms, that it would more properly be called "the history of early Christian religion."[25] Anything that adopts this dictum as a canon will neglect the theological content that I have suggested is necessary. And the practice of basing a biblical theology not on biblical texts but on hypothetical Ur-sources, oral stages, or apocryphal material misses the point of the modifier *biblical*. In short, the terms *biblical* and *theology* serve to mark out the boundaries within which the argument will be conducted, and we may decline to consider works that argue outside those boundaries.

Next, we may call upon the same criteria we use in general theological evaluation. If something is unsatisfactory about a proposed Christology, we may respond by noting that it is docetic, subordinationist, triumphalist, or whatever.[26] There is no dearth of such bases for evaluation, but these have the practical disadvantages of being relatively unfamiliar to biblical scholars and of crossing ingrained disciplinary boundaries.

AESTHETICS AND ETHICS

Finally, I direct your attention to two further kinds of criteria, which we may call aesthetic and ethical (or political) criteria. The aesthetic criterion asks, "Is this fitting (or 'appropriate')?" The second poses the question, "Can we live by this biblical theology?" These may in the end be two ways of asking the same question, but perhaps you can imagine adopting a biblical theology that is in some areas inelegant, or admiring the qualities of a theology by which one could never live.

The point here is not whether these are one or two criteria, but that these questions focus our judgment toward grounds for evaluating biblical theologies. These criteria are open to the objection that they are too subjective. My response is simply that no one makes ethical or aesthetic judgments outside the context of social groups and traditions that define areas within which the supposedly dangerous aspect of subjectivity ebbs away. We are responsible for our judgments, and the kinds of account we offer to justify such judgments will appeal to intersubjective criteria.

HISTORICAL CRITICISM

With all this I do not propose to throw out historical criticism altogether. The influence of historical criticism is to some extent simply inescapable for most interpreters. I simply want to stress that the degree to which historical criticism is the source of legitimation for biblical theology is determined not by the dictates of modern reason, but on the basis of prior judgments about the importance of history to theology. Ernst Käsemann, for instance, argued the necessity of historical foundations for theological interpretations on the grounds that any other course would lead to Docetism.[27] Likewise, it has been suggested that a position such as that defended here would nurture a new Gnosticism, in which illuminati come up with spiritual interpretations that elude carnal readers. One might also argue that historical-critical arguments are necessary for strategic reasons, such as to persuade an audience that is committed to historical-critical canons of truth. While I dispute all of these arguments, I agree that this is the ground on which we should work out our differences—here, on theological grounds, rather than on the premise that historical knowledge is a necessary prerequisite for understanding, or that nonhistorical interpretation is simply retrogressive or uncritical.[28]

Conclusion

If you grant that the criteria for legitimate biblical theology are indeed contingent, and if you recall that theological construals of the Bible are fairly often marginalized for being insufficiently attuned to the historical situation of the text, you will perhaps have jumped ahead of me to the conclusion that one promising place to begin our inquiry into alternatives to modernity's hegemony is in the margins of modern biblical-theological discourse. One outstanding example of such a marginalized discourse is the powerful biblical theology of liberation being pressed by Central and South American theologians; other examples include the efforts to develop nonracist and nonpatriarchal biblical theologies.[29] And although the canonical approach to theology, closely identified with Brevard Childs, maintains a strong historical influence, it, too, might flourish in a nonmodern scholarly atmosphere.

Without taking the time to analyze current enterprises in each of these fields, I will venture to point out that each has devoted considerable energy to legitimating itself with respect to modernity's standards. To the extent that biblical theologians of liberation, feminism, and canonical hermeneutics are themselves committed to the canons of modernity, this is all right; but if feminists adopt these modern standards, they have already committed themselves to developing a feminist biblical theology *only so far as modernity allows*—and modern biblical studies have shown themselves to be none too helpful on this count. And modern scholarship is no more committed to liberation or to proclaiming the faith of the church than it is committed to overcoming patriarchal structures.

The thesis defended here is not that we should abandon historical criticism when developing a biblical theology; since historical criticism is involved—in nontrivial ways—with such fundamental tasks as translation and text criticism, we could not escape recourse to historical-critical research even if we wanted to. I simply claim that there is no necessary reason for making historical criticism the definitive authority for our biblical theologies. While a nonmodern biblical theology may have good reason for making *some* historical claims, there is no inherent need for these claims to lie at the center of biblical theology or for the construal itself to be based on a historical reconstruction.

The strength of the greatest biblical theologies, after all, lies not in their historical analysis (though it may be rigorous), but in the theological penetration and insight of their construals of the Bible. If we would venture to resuscitate the project of biblical theology, we ought to take this as a clue, and if we offer as compelling an exposition of the gospel as did Augustine or John Calvin or Rudolf Bultmann, we will be able to afford to let the historical chips fall where they may.

CHAPTER TWO

Why Historical Criticism Can't Protect Christological Orthodoxy: Reflections on Docetism, Käsemann, and Christology

The market for historical Jesuses has never been hotter. Recently the bookstore shelves have been filled with a mob of Jesus books, whose authors star on videotapes, chat on radio talk shows, and appear on transcontinental live video programs. While interest in Jesus flourishes, however, there is no consensus about what Jesus was really like. The scholars who have landed mass-market publishers are not necessarily the most widely respected representatives of their fields of inquiry; indeed, there is considerable scholarly resistance to the recent spate of Jesuses.[1]

This raises a question: If the experts on historical research arrive at such starkly different pictures of Jesus, why do we care so much about the "historical Jesus"? One common answer is that historical research—the historical-critical method—brings us closer to the real, actual truth about Jesus. Some argue that the church's theological portraits of Jesus have obscured his true character and that the academy's historical analysis will dispel these ecclesiastical distortions. This supposition provides a particular example of one of the theoretical commonplaces of contemporary theological hermeneutics: the claim that historical-critical research is a necessary prerequisite for theological interpretation, lest one's interpretation drift into the heretical terrain of Docetism.[2] Ernst Käsemann, for one, has argued that historical criticism is necessary because it breaks through the Docetism that (he claims) dominates the Christian community.[3] If we examine this axiom closely, however, we will uncover fatal problems with it, problems that will point us toward comparable problems with the notion that the "historical Jesus" might be the real, flesh-and-blood Nazarene.

To show the problems inherent in the historical-critical project (as exemplified by portraits of the historical Jesus), I will examine the apotropaic quality of historical criticism by trying to delineate Docetism more clearly (in both its ancient and contemporary forms), then by examining the extent to which historical criticism can protect theology from these Docetisms. Finally, I will examine the consequences first of *privileging* historical criticism and then of demoting historical criticism from its primacy.

Docetism

When we examine the value of historical criticism as a protection from Docetism, we first encounter grave difficulties in ascertaining the nature of Docetism itself. The *Oxford Dictionary of the Christian Church* alerts us to this problem when it refers to Docetism as "a *tendency*, rather than a formulated and unified doctrine."[4] The earliest Christian polemicists ascribed this "tendency" to a bewildering variety of opponents, and—as we are not surprised to learn—none seems to have embraced or expounded a consistent doctrine of Docetism. The historical sources from which we might elicit a definition of Docetism are on one hand colored by polemical aims and on the other inconsistent and contradictory. Docetism is, as Norbert Brox observes, "a problematic designation."[5]

Michael Slusser points out that Irenaeus describes at least seven groups of his opponents as "docetic."[6] The common characteristic of these groups was their claim that Jesus was not what he seemed to be. Simon Magus, for example, claimed that Jesus had been Simon himself, who "had descended, transfigured and assimilated to powers and principalities and angels, so that he might appear among humans to be a human, while he yet was not a human; and thus he was thought to have suffered in Judaea, when he had not suffered" (*Haer.* 1.23.3).[7] The Basilideans claimed that the

Nous, embodied as Jesus, exchanged identities with Simon of Cyrene, so that Simon was crucified instead of Jesus (while Jesus/Nous stood by, mocking; 1.24.4). Irenaeus mentions a third group of heretics only in passing, admitting that some "describe him as being human only in appearance" (2.22.4). He attributes to some undifferentiated Gnostics the claim that the Son "never became incarnate, nor suffered, but that he descended like a dove on the dispensational Jesus; and that, as soon as he had declared the unknown Father, he did again ascend into the Pleroma" (3.11.2–3). Irenaeus likewise notes that others claimed that Jesus "did become incarnate, and suffered, whom they represent as having passed through Mary just as water through a tube" (3.11.2–3).[8] Slusser concludes that although Irenaeus's opponents manifestly differed in the details of their affirmation, they shared the certainty that Jesus had an occult identity that distinguished him from anything like "full humanity."

The difficulty with Slusser's argument—for our purposes—is that Irenaeus evidently did not know these heretics *as Docetists*, but simply as Simonians, Basilideans, Marcionites, and so on. Hippolytus and Tertullian amplified the portraits of these Christologies, sometimes at considerable length, but did not associate them with "Docetism." Clement of Alexandria knew the Docetists as a group who derived their name from their doctrine, but he believed them to have been founded by Julius Cassian, the Encratite whom he associated principally with rigorous sexual asceticism.[9] He went on, however, to describe both Marcion and Julius Cassian as Docetists on the basis that both describe birth as evil.[10] Hippolytus offered an extended discussion of "those who call themselves 'docetae'": they espoused a complicated ontology of Æons, who collectively generated an offspring in the virgin Mary. This offspring was equal to the Æons in greatness but differed from them inasmuch as he was begotten, whereas the Æons were unbegotten. This redeemer received a second, spiritual body when he was baptized, so that the spiritual body could overcome the physical body at the crucifixion (*Haer.* 8.1–3). These claims lie close to what heresiologists conventionally call Docetism, yet we should notice that the weight of Hippolytus's report, both here and in 10.12, is on the scheme and number of Æons; he mentions the christological claims that we customarily see as specifically docetic only in passing. Serapion's letter on the Gospel of Peter is no more helpful; he does not specify why "we call [these false teachers] Docetists," nor does he say what the docetic aspects of the Gospel of Peter were.[11]

In other words, the patristic heresiologists who discussed Docetism by name held varying views on what Docetists believed, and none of them seems particularly to have associated Docetism with any specific quasi-incarnational Christology.

Of course, the foundation of our familiar definitions of Docetism comes from the Johannine literature and from the letters of Ignatius. Käsemann chastised the "naïve Docetism" he found in John's Gospel; John depicts not a realistic incarnation, but the glorious manifestation of God:

> In what sense is he flesh, who walks on the water and through closed doors, who cannot be captured by his enemies, who at the well of Samaria is tired and desires a drink, yet has no need of drink and has food different from that which his disciples seek? He cannot be deceived by men, because he knows their innermost thoughts even before they speak. He debates with them from the vantage point of the infinite difference between heaven and earth. He has need neither of the witness of Moses nor of the Baptist. He dissociates himself from the Jews, as if they were not his own people, and he meets his mother as the one who is her Lord. He permits Lazarus to lie in the grave for four days in order that the miracle of his resurrection may be more impressive. And in the end the Johannine Christ goes victoriously to his death of his own accord.[12]

The christological tendencies to which Käsemann points in the Fourth Gospel evidently erupt into theological extravagance among the "anti-Christs" of whom the Johannine epistles speak. The epistles' author feels obliged to stress the material corporeality of Jesus ("what we have looked at and *touched with our hands*," 1 John 1:1), his anatomical normality ("[He] came by water and blood, . . . not with the water only but with the water and the blood," 5:6),[13] his physical incarnation ("Jesus Christ has come in the flesh," 4:2; "Many deceivers have gone out into the world, those who do not confess that Jesus Christ has come in the flesh," 2 John 7). Though the implied counter-position—that Jesus was intangible, that he did not have blood, that he did not come in the flesh—makes no explicit reference to the characteristics by which Hippolytus or Clement identified Docetism nor lays claim to the designation of "Docetism," it has been taken as a statement of the fundamental tenets of *dogmengeschichtliche* Docetism.

Likewise the case of Ignatius: He polemicizes against those who teach that Christ "suffered in appearance" (*To the Trallians* 10.1; *Smyrnaeans* 2.1, 4.2) and specifically uses the word *dokein*, from which Docetism draws its name. Yet he does not identify these "unbelievers" as Docetists. There is one point of contact between Ignatius's polemics and the doctrines of the patristic Docetists: in *To the Trallians*, Ignatius stresses that Jesus was "truly born" (9.1), which one might read as a rebuttal of Julius Cassian's sort of Docetism. That point, however, offers only limited help in ascertaining a general definition of Docetism.

We are left on one hand with a fairly distinct christological tendency that cannot be tied firmly to groups whom the patristic writers thought docetic, and on the other hand with a miscellany of putatively docetic doctrines. Slusser and Brox each resolve this dilemma by ingeniously conflating the two groups. Slusser's historical Docetists "denied that in Jesus Christ the divine Savior was truly the subject of all the human experiences of the historical man."[14] Brox concludes that the most fitting definition of Docetism—one that takes

account of the varying accounts of Docetism in the patristic
literature but also attends to the use of the term in contemporary theology—is that "docetism is found where a christology tries to say: Jesus was other than what he seemed to
be."[15] Since we lack decisive evidence, this sort of harmonizing is understandable, though the result elides an important historical problem. The *dogmengeschichtliche* definition
of Docetism that emerges from Slusser's and Brox's efforts
echoes Baur's definition from the early nineteenth century:
The docetic Christ was not what he seemed to be. Though
he seemed to be fully human, this was only an apparent
humanity, which concealed a divine nature, which was conceived either as a second nature or as his own true nature.

These classical Docetisms are clearly inimical to orthodox theology, but does a threat from the heresies that they
represent warrant our establishing historical criticism as a
guardian of contemporary orthodoxy? By no means. In the
first place, historical criticism has been of only limited help
in ascertaining what these heretical tendencies were. More
to the point, it has been enormously helpful in clarifying
how little we know about what "Docetism" meant to the
early heresiologists. This is the historian's job: to represent
our past to us clearly and responsibly. We would be making
a category error were we to ask historians' research now to
defend incarnational Christology (as historical critics working in biblical studies have long insisted within their own
domain). If historians can help correct doctrinal errors, it is
principally by providing reliable historical assessments that
in some way contribute to the doctrinal argument. Historians may thus identify ancient heresies more precisely, show
the consequences of particular beliefs, or recover persuasive
arguments that have been used against such errors by earlier theologians. But by the same token, historical-critical
method cannot suppress, for example, the extent to which
early theologians and texts *support* doctrines that were subsequently deemed heretical (cf. the Gospels' tendency toward
adoptionist Christologies), nor can it suppress the positive

effects that heretical doctrines might have had (such as the high moral standards that many heretics exemplified or the egalitarianism of many heretical movements), nor ignore the persuasive arguments that the ancient heretics might have used. Historical critics cannot play favorites in disputes between orthodox and heterodox parties. In short, historical criticism is constitutively ill suited for a role as *defensor fidei* (defender of the faith).[16]

This controversy's christological focus marks another weakness of historical criticism: historical reason can tell us nothing of the character of Christ's divinity. Historians can tell us about what various theologians, political figures, texts, and images *say* about Christ, but the historiographic ascesis that can immeasurably help clarify interpretive questions also obliges historians to remain mute on a question for which the evidence is inaccessible or (at the very least) fundamentally controverted. What would constitute historical evidence regarding whether Christ was divine on Chalcedonian terms or simply a divine being inhabiting a human appearance? Or whether Christ had a *physical* or *spiritual* body? Here historical critics lack the sorts of evidence and arguments that permit them to draw the conclusions that would, presumably, help confound Docetism.

Thus, classical Docetism—whatever the precise details of one's definition of it—entails claims about Christ's nature and origins that historical criticism simply can't argue. While historians may contribute to the orthodox resistance of Docetism, their methodological neutrality and their rules of evidence and argument undermine any possible claim that their critical works are a necessary prophylaxis against classically docetic errors.

The historical critics have one last, best line of defense. They can still point out that a theologian's hesitation to investigate Jesus according to the rules of historical inquiry already implies the fear that "the way Jesus really was" might contradict some cherished dogmatic principle. On this account, historical criticism is not theologically neutral but is positively necessary in order to exorcise the impression that historical truth might contradict dogma. Historical criticism protects us from the habit of isolating our theological judgments from critical judgments about history. The conspiracy of silence by which clergy and academics protect the theologically fragile laity itself mandates the necessity of historical scholarship.

One difficulty with that position lies in the fallacious assumption that accounts that would disturb "simple believers' faith" are inherently more probable than accounts that would affirm believers' faith. The proclivity of contemporary Christians to believe or disbelieve a given historical account should—as a thoughtful historian ought to recognize—be utterly irrelevant to the account's likelihood.

Moreover, the conspiracy of silence argument implies that academic historians are less likely to be motivated by partisanship or ideology than are theologians. It assumes that historical scholarship renders surer, purer truths than does theological scholarship. Such claims rest on thin air; historians are just as likely to construct an image of Jesus that suits their academic social setting as theologians are likely to construct a Jesus who suits their ecclesiastical setting. Indeed, the present generation of Jesus-questers have begun publishing apologias for their research, and these rationales generally incorporate explicitly theological justifications for their historical research. Moreover, these very justifications are frequently quite at odds with orthodox theology—a very odd circumstance, if historical-critical inquiry is presumed to uphold orthodoxy.

In the end, though, historical interpretation lacks the distinctive capacity to detect and root out Docetism that alone could warrant enshrining historical exegesis as the primary criterion of the church's interpretation of Scripture. Classical Docetism does indeed pose a threat to theologically sound readings, but we avoid these dangers by Chalcedonian interpretation, not by a historical rigor that is constrained in principle to examine only Christ's humanity.

Critics

Does historical criticism prove any more useful for combating the sorts of Docetism that prompted Käsemann's judgment that historical criticism is a necessary preventive measure against the Docetism that dominates the Christian community?[17] The answer depends somewhat on whether the *dogmengeschichtliche* definition of Docetism corresponds to the theological mistake that Käsemann repudiates under the same name. Käsemann, the preeminent exemplar of anti-docetic historicism, uses the term *docetic* in almost as various and complex an assortment of contexts as did the patristic polemicists. He certainly does not use the term to refer exclusively to the error of positing that Jesus' incarnation was only apparent. While he generally uses the term in this sense in his exegetical reflections (for example, on John), his methodological writings use the term freely and unsystematically.

When Käsemann is defending the theological justification of historical criticism, he tends to treat Docetism as a generic danger of soft-pedaling historical inquiry. In various situations, he associates Docetism with biblical inerrantism, resistance to critical questioning, supernaturalistic theology, and approaches to biblical and doctrinal problems that seek to harmonize, rather than sharpen, differences. Though he may be right to warn his audience that these theological approaches are hazardous, it is not clear that they constitute "Docetism"; at least, Käsemann does not make his rationale explicit. At the same time, a particular constellation of assumptions does in fact undergird Käsemann's position, and it does bear some resemblance to Docetism.

For example, Käsemann associates Docetism with the notion that the Bible is "a book fallen from heaven."[18] In other words, he criticizes the inclination to take the Bible as inerrant, as divine communication without any human flaws: "Those who hold the canon to be without error of any kind, perfectly evangelical, inspired in whole and parts alike, have a docetic understanding of it."[19] While this is not a christological question at all, still Käsemann draws a reasonable comparison between the theological claim that Jesus the Messiah was fully human as well as fully divine and a doctrine of Scripture that apparently denies full humanity to the production of the Bible. It is not an exact comparison; there is no ecumenical dogma that defines the nature of the Bible with the same clarity with which the Chalcedonian definition describes the nature of Christ (and Käsemann's opponents might want to argue that just as the fully human Jesus was without sin, so their understanding of the Bible's "humanity" legitimately excludes the possibility of biblical error). Käsemann's usage in this case seems plausible, if imprecise.

Moreover, Käsemann, in a familiar Lutheran fashion, adds the charge of "enthusiasm" to his accusations of Docetism.[20] These charges do not themselves clarify Käsemann's use of the term *Docetism*, however. Käsemann's enthusiastic/docetic interlocutors hold several different positions. They "renounce the truth that revelation takes place on earth and in the flesh."[21] They support a "trusting" or "pneumatic" theology, confusing mission and propaganda and binding Christians to fictions about God and humanity.[22] They eliminate the distinctiveness of Jesus and replace their reverence for the incarnate Lord with worship of a generalized redeemer figure, or even a symbol of God-consciousness.[23] Käsemann's case for associating Docetism with "enthusiasm" may be justified by the traditional association of Docetism with Gnosticism, and of Gnosticism with "enthusiasm." At the same time, Brox has shown that Gnosticism and Docetism can be distinguished as theological and historical phenomena.[24] Though some Gnostics may hold docetic Christologies (as Marcion evidently did, and as Valentinian and Basilidean gnostics were alleged to have done), certainly not all Docetists have been Gnostics, and we sacrifice discursive clarity when we conflate the two phenomena.

Enthusiasm and inerrantism are not the only errors Käsemann sees in Docetism. He also argues that today's

Docetists harmonize theological differences too easily, that they prefer to gloss over fundamental problems in the interest of a superficial harmony. "Only Docetism can afford to ignore the fact that Jacob and Esau live in constant proximity without ever becoming one, and the scandal of the Cross awakes the old Adam simultaneously with the new."[25] Presumably, Käsemann feels that interpretations that effect harmonious reconciliation of texts in which he sees an acrimonious divergence ("Jacob and Esau") are guilty of docetic hermeneutics. Even when Docetists acknowledge difference, such as the tension between humiliation and exaltation of Christ, Käsemann alleges that they evacuate that tension of its content.[26] Käsemann locates the conflict-in-community of Esau and Jacob, of old and new Adam, at the center of sound theology. The tension that docetic interpreters relax and the differences they allegedly elide are at the heart of the Christian proclamation, according to Käsemann.

Here Käsemann is close to the *dogmengeschichtliche* definition of Docetism outlined in the previous section, but he is still carrying his polemics beyond any historically warranted description of Docetism. Docetists were not troubled by the problem of *tension* between divinity and humanity, or humiliation and exaltation; they were troubled by the theological implications of God's taking on flesh, and they addressed those problems by denying the full carnality of the incarnation. They did so not in the interest of glossing over differences, of permitting Jacob and Esau to coexist, but in the interest of protecting the transcendent God from undivine contact with carnal reality. If Käsemann wants to identify this thoroughgoing commitment to divine transcendence with a generalized impulse to stifle difference, he must reckon with the possibility that he himself is eliding important differences.

Perhaps the most important problem that Käsemann sees in his docetic opponents is their refusal to exercise critical judgment. Käsemann cannot abide the possibility that biblical interpretation might involve a *sacrificium intellectus* (sacrifice of the intellect) by which modern disciples are asked to believe claims about the Bible that they have strong reasons to doubt. He sees historical criticism as a means for ensuring that the faithful are not compelled to believe the dubious, buy cheap illusions as historical facts, and conform themselves to illusions about God, humanity, and authority.[27] This end is certainly desirable in the light of the popularity of plastic-Jesus superhero Christologies, but Käsemann's line of resistance may be neither sound nor effective. Once again, we must see that, laudable as Käsemann's aims may be, there is little direct connection between anti-intellectualism in the modern church and historical or dogmatic Docetism. Here, even the metaphorical sense of Docetism is stretched to the breaking point.

In fact, Käsemann's contemporary Docetism and *dog-mengeschichtliche* Docetism are distinct phenomena united only by a vague family resemblance. Käsemann warns against an anti-intellectual, triumphalist, "enthusiastic" resistance to critical inquiry; the patristic theologians, in contrast, struggled against a Christology that denied the full humanity of Christ in the interest of preserving God's transcendence. Yet the Docetists of the early centuries were precisely the intellectuals who perceived the radical incongruity of a divine Person in human flesh, while many of today's anti-intellectual believers hold fiercely to the actual, personal humanity of their Lord. The two *anti*-Docetisms share a concern with the truth of the incarnation; the two Docetisms have relatively little in common except to the extent that both threaten Christ's true humanity.[28] The sole common trait that connects ancient and modern Docetisms abides in a metaphorical identification of the historical Docetists—whose disdain for matter, flesh, and sexuality was so strong that they felt obliged to keep their God separate from actual contact with material reality—with contemporary theologians who resist historical investigation into the life of Jesus, and whose Christologies supposedly lack flesh and blood.

One might imagine that historical criticism would fare especially well against the more modern version of Docetism. If Käsemann has described contemporary theological errors as "Docetism" not literally but in a metaphorical sense, then one would expect historical criticism to refute the contemporary errors more adequately than it addresses classical Docetism. Once again, however, historical criticism is not the panacea that its defenders suppose. Käsemann's opponents are not suffering from a lack of historical criticism; instead, they have quite different criteria for their historical judgments.

Thus, the call for enthusiasts and pietists to devote themselves to historical-critical exegesis misses the mark. Käsemann's opponents are already practicing historical interpretation. His objection is, in effect, that their standards in criticism are different from his or, one may suppose, that their criticism isn't really "critical" enough. This claim differs, though, from the claim that historical criticism protects interpreters against modern Docetism, and Käsemann does not offer an explicit critique of his opponents' criteria. Unless "historical criticism" means only "Ernst Käsemann's approved sort of interpretation," historical criticism can no more remedy modern Docetism than it could cure the classical sort.

Historical Criticism as Theological Prophylaxis

The two Docetisms entail two different errors in theological reasoning. On one hand, the ancient Docetists saw an important distinction between the humanity of Jesus of Nazareth and God's divinity, such that the divinity and humanity were inimical to one another. On the other hand, Käsemann's modern Docetists deny the internal tensions in Scripture in favor of a harmonized inerrant Bible (on the basis of their enthusiastic pietism rather than on sound critical grounds), thus substituting an imagined/desired Jesus for the real human.

Käsemann sees historical criticism as a necessary weapon against his opponents because he evidently takes this form of biblical interpretation as a discourse with privileged access to the truth about Jesus; historical criticism is "scientific" or "scholarly" in ways that other approaches to theological interpretation are not.[29] This assumption, however, may not be strong enough to sustain careful examination. If one wants to privilege the results of historical inquiry, one will need to make a case that historical methods are surer avenues to the truth than are the investigative modes of other fields of inquiry. Just how does historical-critical questioning get us closer to the flesh-and-blood humanity of Jesus than, for example, careful theological reflection does?[30]

To be fair to Käsemann, one should note that he was furiously trying to devise a way to pursue theological interpretation between the bitterly opposed poles of Rudolf Bultmann's demythologized existential interpretation (on one hand) and fundamentalist pietism (on the other).[31] Thus, Käsemann's insistence on historical-critical construction of a flesh-and-blood Jesus resists a Bultmannian inclination to dispense with Jesus in favor of the kerygma, and his insistence on the internal conflict within the New Testament resists the fundamentalists' inclination to posit a uniformly harmonious inspiration guaranteeing the truth of the text. Käsemann may have been right on both counts; his rhetoric, however, suggests the tumult of ideological conflict more than careful analysis of Docetism, Bultmann, fundamentalism, and historical-critical hermeneutics. Critics who sympathize with Käsemann's aims—as many contemporary historicist interpreters do—need to avoid the pitfalls of simply repeating his rhetoric, for Käsemann's case is a good deal weaker than his prose.

One need not undertake a thorough methodological analysis to see a first grave problem with the historical critics' apologetics. If historical-critical reconstruction presents us with a more *real*, more truly carnal Jesus than does every other approach to biblical interpretation, then just which Jesus is

the real, carnal one? Was Jesus a peripatetic Mediterranean
Cynic? Was he a doomsaying apocalyptic prophet? Was he a
Galilean Jewish miracle worker or a Hellenistic magician? If
he was, say, a Cynic philosopher, then the historical accounts
that purport to demonstrate that Jesus is best understood
as a Galilean holy man no more represent the real, carnal
Jesus than does a Docetist's theological projection. But if the
historians who advocate the Galilean-holy-man Christology
are right, the Cynic-philosopher historians have constructed
an unreal phantasm. If historical-Jesus research protects us
from erroneous judgments about Jesus' real, carnal humanity, how are we to protect ourselves from erroneous historical accounts?

Historical-critical apologists must confront an even larger
problem, however. Classical and contemporary Docetists
share the error of displacing the real, human Jesus in favor of
an image based on presuppositions about what Jesus *must have
been like*; early Docetists knew that the Savior must have been
so divine that he could have had no actual humanity, and current Docetists presumably base their understanding of Jesus
on a sort of idealized gentle twentieth-century Alan Alda figure. The historical apologists must show that their research-
ers are less prone to this error than are non-historical-critical
interpreters. Of course, one implication of Albert Schweitzer's
Quest of the Historical Jesus (and of many subsequent articles)[32]
is precisely that historical critics are every bit as prone to this
error as are their theologically interested colleagues. Historical
criticism may serve a limited function in this regard—pointing out that Jesus would not have used a transistor radio and
did not speak in King James's English—but historical method
cannot give greater assurance regarding what Jesus was like
than does theological reflection. Indeed, since "Docetism" is
a phenomenon defined and applied by specifically theological
discourses, one might well suppose that theologians are especially well situated to identify and avoid this error.

The historical apologists' position faces several built-in
problems. First, any of our images of Jesus—historical or

theological or psychological—is always constrained by particular definitions of plausibility. Judgments deemed plausible at sessions of the Society of Biblical Literature might not be deemed plausible at meetings of the House of Bishops, for example (and certainly vice versa). Defenders of historical criticism have not, however, presented an adequate explanation of why their sort of plausibility provides a more suitable defense against Docetism than does an alert theological sensitivity to dis-incarnating Jesus. Once again, historical critics and theologians alike show a strong tendency to describe a Jesus tailored to fit their own presuppositions. In a word, historical criticism does not necessarily provide sturdier or more "real" flesh for our images of Jesus than does careful theological imagination. Of course, part of the historian's defense is that she may be wrong about just what Jesus was like, but she is bound (by the plausibility-criteria characteristic of historical criticism) to have produced an image of Jesus that was at least fully human. By concentrating on the aspects of Jesus' career that are amenable to historical assessment, the historian guarantees that she will not describe a divine being who had no contact with human flesh. At this point, however, one may well wonder whether the danger of imagining an insufficiently human Jesus outweighs the risk of prescribing an Ebionite, purely human Jesus who bears no imprint of the divine.[33]

Second, no image of Jesus will ever be more than a construction, whether a historical construction or a theological construction—and both sorts are equally real (or unreal), and each sort is implicated in the other. The historical construct cannot claim greater "reality" or "truth" than any other; it can claim no more than that it appeals to the same kinds of evidence and warrants as those our particular intellectual world customarily relies on for accounts about Tiberius or Mo Tzu. Such a claim, however, fails to address the pivotal questions of both classical and contemporary Docetisms. With regard to both Docetisms, a historical approach stipulates preconditions that themselves constitute aspects of the problem. Classical Docetism entails ambiguity about the relation of the divine and human natures of Christ, but the discipline of modern historical inquiry rigorously excludes speculation on divine agency and identity. Contemporary Docetism entails ambiguity about the sources of reliable information concerning Jesus' true flesh-and-blood identity, but modern historical inquiry ignores the voices of those who do not already have credentials as modern historical scholars (thus effectively limiting the criteria for Jesus' flesh-and-blood identity to conventional historical rules). The historians' Jesus is as much a projection of their historical imaginations as any theologian's Jesus is a projection of a theological imagination.

Historical criticism works as theological prophylaxis against Docetism only for those theologians who both accept the authority of historical inquiry and find themselves tempted to expound images of Jesus that diverge radically from any human being who might have lived in the first century. Those who dispute the historians' authority will not take the medicine Käsemann prescribes, and those who already accept a Jesus who fits more or less smoothly into what we surmise about the first-century world derive no further benefit from the historical criticism.

Benign Precaution
or Malign Constriction?

Not only does the practice of historical-critical interpretation not protect its adherents from docetic errors, but it has certain distinctly malignant side effects. The first is its proclivity to self-righteous exclusion of any alternative ways of reading. So it is that Robert Grant and David Tracy's *Short History of Biblical Interpretation*, Robert Morgan and John Barton's *Biblical Interpretation*, and John Rogerson, Christopher Rowland, and Barnabas Lindars's *Study and Use of the Bible*[34] are principally histories of the development of academic historical criticism, with scarcely a word about

(for two prominent examples) the African-American interpretive tradition or fundamentalist interpretations. Moreover, historical-critical authorities' hegemony has produced
a strong bias in favor of "readers like us," interpreters who
reproduce the customary historical-critical interpretive,
deliberative interests and rhetorical tactics. This production (and reproduction) of historical-critical readers has
relegated other readers—untrained in academic criticism
and frequently resistant to what they perceive as historical
criticism's own hidden gender, racial, and political agenda—
to intellectual nonexistence. If Käsemann can persuade
his colleagues that the alternative to rigorously historical
inquiry amounts to intellectual condescension, enthusiasm,
and bibliolatry, and that it leads to the heresy of Docetism,
then few academic interpreters will show even faint interest in the possibility of legitimate theological interpretation
apart from historical-critical foundations.

One ought not read the foregoing critique as an assault
on historical inquiry per se; there are many important reasons contemporary interpreters ought to acquaint themselves with the discipline and literature of historical criticism.
Many great theological and biblical expositions have been
written at least in dialogue with, if not under the guidance
of, historical criticism. Moreover, many interpreters do lead
their lives and order their intellectual priorities in such a way
that a historical-critical outlook constitutes a fundamental
aspect of their identity; their lives bespeak a commitment to
the version of "truth" knit together in the womb of modern
culture. Were these modern interpreters to make a special
exception when they read the Bible, they might indeed be
sacrificing their intellectual integrity.

Yet there are also many interpreters who have not mildly
accepted the authority of the critics. They may resist historical criticism altogether or relegate it to an ancillary role in
their interpretive repertoire. They may simply neither know
nor care about the rules and results of historians' research.
But one cannot justify the argument that such interpreters

(already quite artificially associated as the Other of histori-cal interpretation) are incipient Docetists. Whatever the strengths and weaknesses of their readings, they do not stand automatically condemned as heretics.

The academic interpreters would in many respects be better off if they dismounted their high horses and attended to nonhistorical interpreters. After all, no *theoretical* account of Jesus will itself be fully incarnational. A dispute over the carnality or Docetism of Jesus that is isolated from prac-tice is a purely *scholastic* question. Anyone who would avoid Docetism would do better to begin by feeding the hungry and clothing the naked than by consulting the most recent historical-Jesus research.

Are the claims that I advance here a recrudescence of Käsemann's anti-intellectual, enthusiastic-pietist Docetism? Possibly so, but readers will allow that the argument of these pages has rested not on claims about the nature of Scripture or about warmly pious feelings regarding Jesus. Instead, I have pressed a case that risks being *overly* intellectual to sug-gest that historical criticism cannot justify claims that it is the only sound theological approach to biblical interpreta-tion or the necessary first step for christological reflection. In any case, historical criticism does not provide a neces-sary (or even an effective) bulwark against either classical or contemporary Docetism. One may have valid intellectual reservations about the value of historical criticism without thereby running the risk of heresy.

CHAPTER THREE

Twisting to Destruction: A Memorandum on the Ethics of Interpretation

During the years in which Dan Via served as my dissertation adviser, he continually pressed me to clarify my hermeneutical claims, particularly with respect to hermeneutical legitimacy and the ethics of interpretation: "Doesn't your claim mean that people can say texts mean anything they want?" This chapter sketches the response still owed to my mentor. His concern that some interpretations are improper addresses the intersection of hermeneutics and ethics, a topic that several scholars have explored in recent books and articles.[1] Though I do not assume that this essay will convince those who share Via's concern, perhaps it may provoke the sophisticated rebuttal that will clarify the hermeneutical issues raised here.

The point that exercised my professor was my insistence that we do not need transcendent criteria for interpretation in order to make judgments with respect to interpretive legitimacy or ethics. Our impulse to uphold particular criteria for interpretation as necessary, natural, or transcendent masks the circumstantial determinations that shape our evaluations. The absence of transcendent criteria is not a loss to lament, however. We do not need (transcendent) criteria that we have never had, but we can safely rely upon the innumerable *local* restrictions by which we can judge biblical interpretations.

The Problem of Transcendent Criteria

This claim is unwelcome in many quarters. Many readers, especially readers of the Bible, want a reliable interpretive method that depends on norms that transcend their specific circumstances, which would thus carry unquestionable authority. If we could find the *right* way to interpret, we could simply apply that correct method to the text and demand that everyone acknowledge our proper interpretations. Misreadings would arise only from deviations from the transcendent interpretive norms; readers might apply the method inappropriately, or misconstrue the method, or apply the method to an inadequate text and thereby generate illegitimate interpretations. This model funds the currency of anthropomorphic metaphors in hermeneutical discourse. When critics conclude that texts "restrain" or "compel" or "suggest" or "invite" interpretations, they mystify their complicity with the text's alleged restraint, compulsion, suggestion, or invitation. When they observe that an interpretation is "unfair" to the text, that it does not "do justice to the text," they tacitly appeal to unquestioned assumptions about the "human rights" of texts.

If texts do not have rights—if the desired transcendent criteria are unavailable—then matters are much more complicated. With no criteria that transcend all the particular formations of reader, text, audience, and social context, our interpretations stand available for assessments by a variety of local ethical criteria. Indeed, could we but see them, scores of criteria are foreign to our lives but vigorous and forceful in their own interpretive neighborhoods. As my professor pointed out, the (posited) absence of transcendent criteria seems to imply that there is no way to judge one interpretation as better than another.

This apparent danger, however, vanishes once we recognize that the phantasm of interpretive anarchy is still a projection of the desire for transcendent criteria. If there are no transcendent criteria, there can be no "interpretive chaos" either. So long as we generate and evaluate interpretations from particular contextual constellations (as we always do), we will never lack criteria for judging interpretations. Indeed, our contextual constellations themselves provide the criteria by which we assess interpretations. One can no more say that a text means whatever one likes than one can say that a red, octagonal road sign means whatever one likes. No transcendent law obliges one to stop at such a sign, but effective local constraints will enforce a particular interpretation of such a sign. Interpretations—of biblical texts as of traffic signs—always have consequences. The constraints upon textual interpretation do not derive from the nature of understanding, or of texts, or of language, or of communicative intent, or of truth, or of speech-acts, but always only from the sundry collocations of circumstances within which we formulate interpretations and judgments.

Interpretation as Social Act

This account implies that interpretive legitimacy is an ineluctably *social* matter. We approve or reject interpretations not on the basis of immutable laws, but on the basis of criteria that we share with particular groups of readers to whom we are accountable. These groups of readers—which we sometimes designate with the collective terms *schools, movements, -isms, interpretive communities,* or *reading formations*[2]—constitute the social embodiment of the interpretive rules they hold. Such groups are not exclusive; interpreters may read by the conventions of different groups at different times, with different texts. When I teach introductory Greek, I urge a simplified model of interpretation wherein certain constructions *must* be construed in certain ways. Once students progress beyond the elementary stages, however, I acquaint them with the less predictable dimensions of Hellenistic Greek. The conventions that constitute groups of readers do not all operate at the same level. Our participation in a community defined by language literacy is usually so easy to presuppose that we do not even regard it as a significant dimension of interpretation. If we acquiesce to poststructuralist literary theories, however, we find ourselves in a much smaller group, whose criteria have less public support. (Likewise, readers in the United States will not be held accountable for misunderstanding a traffic sign printed in

Chinese, but they will be held accountable for arguing that the sign's meaning was indeterminate.) Finally, these sets of interpreters are in constant flux; readers abandon their commitments to one body of interpretive conventions in favor of another, while the conventions that constitute the groups are themselves slowly changing. There are no fixed stars in this hermeneutical universe.

The simplest way of expressing the preceding observations is this: the legitimacy of an interpretation is determined by the body of readers evaluating it.[3] Certain interpretations are, as it were, "at home" in certain reading formations; that is to say, the interpretations in question conform to the conventions by which the group operates. Since reading formations exercise varying degrees of influence upon varying readers, the extent to which readings are at home may involve complicated negotiations among interpretive priorities. Consider the example of a skeptical judgment on the historicity of a particular saying of Jesus. Such an interpretation will be more at home in a liberal university's divinity school than in a conservative seminary. But it will remain more at home in the conservative seminary's academic setting than in a tent revival, since the particular interpretation will be based on the discursive premises and couched in the academic language shared by the university and seminary.

All this being the case, the problem of interpretive legitimacy concerns not so much *whether* there are criteria by which we can judge interpretations, but *which* criteria we apply. Such a problem has no universal answer. The answers we give at particular times to the particular people who ask us about interpretive legitimacy will depend on the reading formations comprising the text, the interpreter, and the audience. Though this sounds giddyingly indeterminate, the implied indeterminacy applies only to the extent that we are considering interpretations in the abstract. Once we examine actual interpreters and actual interpretations, the local constraints on interpretation become starkly obvious.

For example, although I might in theory propound to my classes and colleagues an interpretation of Matthew as a numerological revelation of the mathematical principles of the cosmos, in practice such an interpretation would be virtually impossible for me. My family and friends would become gravely concerned for my sanity. The publishers with whom I am accustomed to dealing would refuse to countenance work that depended upon such an outré premise and would probably hesitate to accept any work at all from an author they regarded as unstable. My colleagues and students would avoid conversation with me. I would probably be relieved of teaching responsibilities as soon as practicable. I would be alienated, destitute, without professional authority; in short, my interpretation will very thoroughly and effectively have been marked as illegitimate.

Now I might persist in my numerological gloss on Matthew and attract a coterie of somewhat off-center supporters—perhaps even a regular column in a weekly tabloid newspaper or appearances on sensationalist television programs. The same interpretations that my former associates and employers had rejected will have become the foundation of my newfound popularity. My extravagant speculations will have *found a home* in the netherworld of popular credulity. The associates who uphold my mathematical Matthew will have no use for my former academic writings (though they will probably make hay of my academic credentials and my persecution by narrow-minded conventional critics). If I tried to gain authority among tabloid-newspaper readers by waving historical-critical exegeses and hermeneutical treatises at them, they would spurn me as just another closed-minded cleric whose brain had been washed by the ecclesiastical authorities' conspiracy to suppress the truth. The work that marks me as a legitimate interpreter in one sphere is useless or detrimental in another.

While these scenarios are possible in the sense that they are within my capacities, they are nearly impossible in the sense that the character who maintains an intellectually demanding relationship with his wife, who was taught by Dan O. Via Jr. at Duke University, who has grown close to a number of trusted colleagues, and who has pastoral responsibilities in the Episcopal Church could hardly behave in such a way—nor could he approve of such an interpretation should someone else propound it.[4] The socially enforced constraints on interpretation effectively inhibit such behavior.

Observe, however, that there is nothing about such prohibition that depends on transcendent rules of interpretation or on the essential nature of textuality or understanding. The restraints on interpretation all operate at the practical, local level. These local restraints differ for each interpreter, so that although I can't produce an algebraic interpretation of Matthew, comparably outlandish interpretations have issued from different reading formations.

Moreover, any judgment on what sort of interpreter someone ought to be will emerge from a context that already favors one outcome or another.[5] Academic readers of this book will favor a more conventional academic author, but if by some chance this chapter were to fall into the hands of some speculative tabloid-believers, they would presumably lend their support to the author of the unfettered mathematical reading. Such a circumstance epitomizes the problem that motivates critics to quest after transcendent criteria: only criteria that transcend the difference that separates academic from tabloid interpreters can justify one sort of interpretation and banish another. If these criteria existed, we might reasonably expect to see their positive influence on interpretive conflict, but instead we see that interpretive "differends" (see note 5) persist undiminished.[6] The persistence of hermeneutical conflict should thus be an empirical sign that no grounds for evaluation escape entanglement in the local reading formations that espouse them. Once again, this should dispel fears that lack of transcendent criteria will launch us into an interpretive twilight zone. There are not, and there never have been, universal criteria to adjudicate interpretive disputes, but the domain of interpretation is no more anarchic than, perhaps, a crowded parking lot—not by any means as orderly as we would desire, but a long way from chaos.

In other words, the local constraints on interpretation—the only ones available—do an adequate job of staving off hermeneutical anarchy and supporting responsible reading. Difficulties emerge when one reading formation demands obeisance from others, as when academic interpreters insist that other sorts of readers should check their interpretations with the "critically responsible" historical interpreters.[7] There is not necessarily a rich enough set of interpretive constraints common to the academic interpreters and the readers whose interpretations they want to control, so the would-be referees are often disqualifying interpretations for violating rules that the interpreter had no intention of acknowledging. More to the point, however, the academic arbiters usually lack the power to execute the truly effective local restraints that I described; instead, they can only issue a stream of denunciations, anathemas, and condescending explanations of how their resistant opponents have gone wrong.

Interpreting Ethically

All of which brings us back to remembering that our acts of interpretation are not ontologically different from our other acts. The ethics of interpretation impinges on people's lives in just the same ways that medical ethics and etiquette impinge on people's lives. This, after all, is the point that the author of 2 Peter makes with respect to his opponents, when he observes that when "the ignorant and unstable" readers interpret Paul's writings, they "twist [them] to their own destruction" (3:16). Peter (or whoever) is not suggesting that the opponents have failed to use the historical-critical method to interpret the letters, nor that they have failed to understand the nature of textuality. He is concerned that the opponents' interpretations issue in licentious and ungodly behavior; there are certainly grounds to associate the errant interpreters with the "false prophets" whom Peter condemns in chapter 2.

Peter's opponents can say that the Pauline letters mean anything they like, but neither they nor Peter can formulate a rule of interpretation that transcends their particular social formations. The debate between Peter and his opponents does not so much concern the rules of interpretation, but rather it concerns the kind of community that will adjudicate claims fittingly to have interpreted Paul's letters and "the other scriptures"; it is a conflict over who defines which interpretations are "at home" in the church. The ecclesial audience judged Peter's side of the conflict more persuasive, not on the basis of transcendent rules of interpretive legitimacy, but on the basis of their vision of what the church's interpretation of its scriptures ought to look like.

Following Peter's example, then, let us recognize that interpretations and differences of interpretation are subject to ethical evaluation. Biblical interpretation has suffered from the long-standing assumption that this hermeneutical discipline is *scientific*, and that (as a consequence) biblical critics are no more subject to criticism for their research and conclusions than are other scientists.[8] Scientific biblical scholars have claimed that, in effect, they are no more subject to ethical criticism for their interpretations than are chemists who interpret the interaction of selenium and oxygen. One's decision to adhere to allegedly scientific academic interpretive practices (aiming at objectivity, practicing the historical-critical method, distancing one's biblical interpretation from the possible influence of the church), however, is not protection against malfeasance. Indeed, Peter would probably count "objective" interpreters among those who are twisting to destruction. On Peter's criteria, Paul's letters should issue in a devotion to God and Christ that produces peace, purity, and patience (2 Peter 3:14–15), not necessarily in proliferating rhetorical analyses and partition theories.

The church's criteria are not ultimate or final, not singular or uncontested; indeed, the very rhetoric of Peter's judgment appeals to the only transcendent judge of interpretation and warns of the eschatological consequences of wrongheaded hermeneutics. However, though neither we nor Peter have access to transcendent interpretive rules, we are not bereft of all criteria. The local criteria to which we have access always provide guidance for ethical (legitimate) interpretation, and these local criteria are much easier to discern if we are not chasing after absent universals in a frustrated search for transcendent criteria.

CHAPTER FOUR
Postmodern Criticism Applied: Matthew's Readers, Power, and Ideology

To qualify as a card-carrying interpreter of the Gospel of Matthew, one must take sides in the ongoing debate over whether Matthew is "anti-Jewish." Fred Burnett has made a great point of this question, asking pointedly, "Is it possible to read Matthew's gospel without an anti-Jewish reading effect?"[1] The question, thus framed, compels our attention; the difficulty is that the very frame of the question is mis-constructed. While no one should minimize the extent to which Matthew's Gospel has been used to justify violence and discrimination against Jews, no more should anyone mistakenly suppose that "anti-Semitism" or "anti-Judaism" is inherent in Matthew. Thus, while I have been well taught to resist anti-Judaism wherever I encounter it, I wish to offer three arguments against the widespread sentiment that Matthew's Gospel is itself anti-Jewish.

The case for my claim rests on theoretical, historical, and practical warrants. The theoretical argument is that a text cannot oblige its interpreters to think in any particular way. Readers' interpretations of texts are constrained not by the texts themselves, but by innumerable social interactions that prescribe and proscribe interpretive possibilities. The historical argument suggests that critics who describe Matthew's polemic with such terms as *anti-Semitism* or *anti-Judaism* are (although perhaps well intentioned) guilty of anachronism and muddy argumentation. Matthew obviously excoriates various Judean parties, but he does so from *within* Judaism, not *over against* Judaism. Finally, the matter of Matthew's supposed anti-Semitism emphasizes one

67

aspect of the Gospel's interpretive history while overlooking another dimension of its *Wirkungsgeschichte* (history of effects). The Gospel of Matthew—widely known as "the Jewish Gospel"—can justify self-denying support of the continuing people of Israel. While the argument that Matthew is anti-Semitic proceeds from laudable sensitivity, it makes the pivotal mistake of scapegoating a ("Jewish") text for the sins of its Gentile readers.

The Theoretical Argument

It is time for us to acknowledge that "texts don't have ideologies."[2] At no point in a text's history, from its original production to any particular subsequent interpretation, may one coherently say the text has been imbued with ideology (any more than the text has a "meaning"[3]). The initial, "original" phase of a text's history might determine the text's ideology; but no single originary moment seems to account for a text's ideology adequately. Even if such a moment existed, our capacity to detect it and pin down the ideological pressures that informed the text at that official *moment* is far from reliable: Stephen Fowl reminds us, "It is often very difficult [he might well say "never possible"] to read back from an ancient textual artifact to the ideological interests behind its production. Such interests can get muted, disguised, or ironically displaced beyond recognition."[4] Moreover, since any given *moment* comprises a variety of conflicting ideological pressures, our effort to chain a text to a moment of ideological crystallization will require us to isolate not only a *moment* of ideological determination, but also one particular ideological vector.[5] The criteria we use to privilege a given moment as originary, and the criteria by which we determine which ideological current constitutes the decisive influence, will themselves always be ideologically overdetermined.

If, instead, one seeks some moment other than the origin at which the text acquires its ideology, one must justify the decision to attribute ideological authority to that particular moment rather than any prior moments. When did the text become ideological? Was the text innocent before then? Do later interpretive epochs ignore or misconstrue the text's own ideology? The effort to impute ideology to texts ensnares interpreters in a mare's nest of theoretical and historical problems. If even the most diligent and suspicious of our interpretive predecessors have overlooked the latent ideology of their texts, what justifies our confidence that we, finally, have attained the high ground that will enable us to see the text's *true* ideology? Fowl's careful deliberations lead him to conclude, "There is no explanatory gain and much conceptual confusion introduced by talking about the ideology of the text."[6] Even my superficial survey of the complexities that this claim entails tends to confirm Fowl's judgment; if texts have ideologies, we are in no position to recognize them, specify their character, or explain how they got there.

The argument so far may seem too purely theoretical. Real-life (*diesseitig*) readers continue to argue about texts' ideologies, and certainly many readers have commented upon the "anti-Jewish" character of Matthew's Gospel. Even more important, many readers have *acted* on the basis of what they concluded were warrants found in Matthew's Gospel for the persecution and execution of Jews. Does my position attribute their claims to theoretical naïveté, or do I concede that there really is some sort of anti-Jewish stratum in the First Gospel?

I certainly do not suppose that if only Matthew's detractors had a better theory, they would recant and commend this Gospel, or that more theoretically sophisticated executioners would have given up their grisly practice. Neither, however, do I concede that someone's claim that "Matthew's Gospel justified my actions" counts as testimony that anti-Jewishness subsists in the text. Rather, people who are already inclined to read a text as anti-Jewish find Matthew a useful document and then "find" in Matthew a warrant for their preexisting condition.

A case illustrating my general point is a pamphlet entitled "The Shortest-Way with the Dissenters," which appeared in Britain in late 1702. The tract rehearsed the history of the Dissenters' role in English history and concluded, "'Tis vain to trifle in this matter, the light foolish handling of them by Mulcts, Fines, &c. If one severe Law were made, and punctually executed, that who eer was found at a Conventicle, shou'd be Banished the Nation, and the Preacher be Hang'd, we shou'd soon see the end of the Tale."[7] The pamphlet was warmly received by High Church opponents of Nonconformity; they read it as a commonsensical call to exterminate the poisonous, cancerous, regicidal forces of ecclesiastical dissent. Only when word leaked out that Daniel Defoe— the popular essayist, known to be a Dissenter himself—had written the pamphlet did the public recognize the text as a satirical essay written *against* the High Church party.

Is "The Shortest-Way" an anti-Dissenter text? Or is it anti-Dissent only when the text omits mention of its author (the phrase *by Daniel Defoe* marking the text as in favor of Toleration)? Nothing *in the text* identifies the genre as satire rather than straightforward political polemic; it does not even propose outlandishly cruel punishments for Dissenters (this was, after all, the early eighteenth century, when a parodist might have proposed that Dissenters be drawn and quartered and that their preachers be flayed alive). Even when one adds Defoe's name to the text of the essay, a reader unaware of Defoe's own ecclesiastical commitments is susceptible to the impression that "The Shortest-Way" simply advocates deportation and hanging as the solution to theological dissent. The text doesn't *have* a theological ideology; rather, readers bring ideologically determined premises to their encounters with the text and produce ideologically freighted interpretations.

The value of the example of Defoe's pamphlet is its strident, unrelenting vituperation against one particular theological/national constituency. "The Shortest-Way" is, in many respects, as unambiguous a political text as one could hope for. The Gospel of Matthew is considerably less one-sided when it considers Judaism. If we have trouble locating "anti-Toleration" in Defoe's essay, might that not count as a sign that we are on still shakier ground when we try to define Matthew as anti-Jewish?

Not only is ideology underdefined in such prominent matters as whether a text promotes or discourages Dissent (or Judaism), but texts are so far from "having" ideologies that one can readily enough find examples of readers who have not considered *either* of the binary alternatives "pro-" or "anti-Judiasm" as truly representing the point of Matthew's Gospel. Theosophists can point to Matthew's intent to guide us to spiritual enlightenment, and one recent author has argued that the Gospel of Matthew—along with the rest of the New Testament—encodes an allegorical description of a pattern of circles and lines that reveals the principles of cathedral architecture, the heliocentric universe, and the origins of the Catholic Mass.[8] Judaism and anti-Judaism are irrelevant to such readers, except to the extent that both alternatives distract from the true significance of the text.

The import of this theoretical argument is that ideology is inherent not in texts, nor even in readers, but in what Tony Bennett calls "reading formations": the intersections of readers with colleagues to whom they are accountable, with texts, and with various other institutional and social constraints on interpretation.[9] No text is ideologically tainted (with or against Judaism, anti-Toleration, bourgeois complacency, or any strain of political inadequacy) without the cooperation of readers and institutions that *construct* the text as "ideologically tainted." Matthew's Gospel is not anti-Jewish unless—until—we make it anti-Jewish.

The Historical Argument

Even if my theoretical arguments have gravely miscarried and my readers are still convinced that it makes some sense to refer to a text as "anti-Jewish," there remain several cogent reasons for doubting that Matthew is an example of anti-Jewish writing. Indeed, the argument that Matthew is anti-Jewish itself draws upon certain (ideological) assumptions that do not withstand close scrutiny.

First, the argument that Matthew is "anti-Jewish" depends on the assumption that Matthew stands for something other than Judaism,[10] meaning Matthean Christianity stands over against something we identify as "Judaism." But such an assumption poses several serious problems. It is not at all clear, first, that Matthew polemicizes against the practices and beliefs that characterize Judaism in general; he may well be criticizing specific constituencies within Judaism without condemning Judaism itself. By the same token, the meanings of even those passages that appear most pointedly to scapegoat Judaism harbor certain ambiguities; Matthew's critics may simply have misunderstood him at crucial points. Finally, contemporary critics commonly work with an anachronistic notion of first-century Judaism, a tendency exacerbated by misleading translations of key terms. In short, the historical case for reading Matthew as anti-Jewish is a good deal weaker than the widely held conviction that Matthew's Gospel belongs "at or near the top of the list" of the most "anti-Jewish" writings of the New Testament.[11]

A burgeoning literature on what Gabriele Boccaccini calls "middle Judaism"—the religion of Israel between the third century BCE and the second century CE—consistently emphasizes that in this period, Judaism was seriously divided precisely over what "Judaism" meant.[12] Numerous scholars now concede that nascent Christianity was one among many first-century Judean contenders for Abraham's heritage. Thus, Christianity was one among many rival "Judaisms."[13] This problem in assuming that Matthew's polemics are anti-Jewish would be akin to saying that Rush Limbaugh's fulminations against Bill Clinton and the Democratic Party mark the talk-show rhetorician as anti-American. Matthew is indeed pointedly critical of

Nonetheless, Matthew's critics adduce much evidence of his anti-Judaism. Matthew's Jesus criticizes Pharisees, Sadducees, scribes, leaders, and priests; Matthew states that the leaders of the people fraudulently claimed that Jesus' body was stolen, not resurrected (lifted, not raised). Matthew reports that "the people as a whole" assented to Jesus' crucifixion with the shout, "His blood be on us and on our children!" (27:25). Matthew's polemics against religious leaders—quite possibly intended to include religious leaders in Matthew's own Christian setting—refer explicitly to priests, Pharisees, and scribes, so readers might conclude that Christian leaders are exempt from such criticism.[16] Of course, Jesus subjects Gentile rulers to pointed criticism as well.

Finally, it is time to recognize that the convention of translating *Ioudaios* as "Jew" or "Jewish" misleadingly inscribes the modern distinction between politics and religion into first-century discourse. Neither historical lexicography nor social-scientific analysis supports this practice. A first-century Judean, like other Judeans, would have been expected to worship the God of Israel. Alexandrian Africans who worshiped the God of Israel were known as Judeans; Gentiles who turned from their families' beliefs became Judeans (they "Judaized"); and inhabitants of Judea who defied local custom by worshiping another god were not, in the proper sense of the word, "Judeans." The anachronistic translation is defensible only in a handful of special cases, and even there only on the assumption that Judaism is already something Other for the New Testament writers. But that is precisely the point in question, and assuming the consequent cannot strengthen translators' cases. The very language in which the "anti-Jewishness" argument is couched suggests that ideological forces are directing the shape of our discussion. Though the scholars who press this case are ostensibly thoroughly historical in their outlook, the resoluteness with which they defend the linguistic distinction between religious identity ("Jew") and national identity

his contemporaries; but he is, in Scot McKnight's word
loyal critic": "Matthew's viewpoint, then, is that of a]
Jew who believes that a new epoch in salvation-his·
dawned in Jesus Christ."[14]

We have evidence for five major theological partie
the first century, each of which proposed a different vi:
of Israel's identity and vocation. Pharisees, Sadducees,]
enes (and the Qumran community, if one takes these to
distinct groups), Samaritans, and Christians all conten
for the prerogative to decide what counted as true faith
ness to the God of Israel. More than one of these gro
resorted to vituperative polemics against others. More tl
one of these groups espoused theologies that relegated otl
contenders to the sidelines of salvation history. It wou
however, sound distinctly odd were we to chastise the De
Sea sect for anti-Judaism, and even odder if we applied t
same criticism to rabbinic Judaism's treatment of Sama
tans. We cannot reasonably apply the label *anti-Jewish*
any of these groups without presupposing that they cou
have known which of the contenders would eventual
attain the status of defining the nature of Judaism.[15] Even
the cataclysm of 70 CE eliminated the Sadducees and Es
enes from the competition—and that assumption oversin
plifies what must have been a more complex process—th
fall of the Temple did not decide the disputes remainin
among Pharisees, Samaritans, and Christians. If we recog
nize that the Judaisms of the first century included othe
less historically prominent alternatives as well, and if w
remember that each of these Judaisms was itself internall
contested, the justification for calling *any* of them anti·
Jewish must become intensely problematic. Matthew (like
other Christians) was certainly distinct from other Judaisms
and probably was unwelcome in most synagogues, but these
distinctions and their concomitant polemics can't be judged
anti-Jewish unless we first contradict Matthew's own conviction that he represented a faithful Judaic witness to the
God of Israel.

("Judean") suggests that their interpretation may be influenced most forcefully by modern liberal political ideology and by their horror of anything resembling anti-Judaism.

Judaism as a distinctively *religious* phenomenon cannot be said to have begun before the second century, before Rome dissolved the temple state that grounded Judean identity. As James Charlesworth has pointed out, "It is simply impossible today to apply the adjective 'Jewish' or 'Christian' to some phenomena prior to approximately 135 C.E."[17] Malina and Rohrbaugh (citing Neusner) push that date even further along, to the fourth century.[18] In the period that Matthew represents—and I am not aware of a persuasive argument for dating Matthew after the bar Kochba revolt—the movements that grew from Jesus' ministry and from subsequent mission to the Gentile world are not distinct from *Judaism*, but from Pharisaism, Essenism, and so on. Burnett, Patte, Levenson, and others do not so much as nod to this matter; they begin with the Matthew–"Jews" dichotomy and work from there. If one's starting point is skewed, however, one's conclusions are bound to be suspect.

If we want to argue that Matthew harbors an anti-*Jewish* ideology, we need to make the case that not only does Matthew reject those particular *divisions* of Judaism that he excoriates, but he has turned his back on the entire complex of characteristics that constitute Judaism, including the legal authority of Torah, the prophetic witness to theological truth, and the pivotal importance of Jerusalem and the Temple. This case would be difficult to make. Matthew's Jesus declares that not one iota or "stroke of a letter" will pass away from the Law (5:18). Matthew places distinctive emphasis on Jesus' continuity with the tradition of the Hebrew Scriptures (especially in the formula-quotations). Finally, Matthew's emphasis on Jesus' primary mission to the lost sheep of the house of Israel (10:6; 15:24) suggests that Matthew was not rejecting Judaism but rather promulgating what he took to be the *correct sort* of Judaism.

The Practical Argument

The most compelling argument in favor of taking Matthew as an anti-Jewish text is not theoretical or historiographic, however, but practical. We know that Christians have long used such texts as Matthew 27:25 ("His blood be on us and our children!") to brand Jews as deicides. We Christians have emphasized the woes against the Pharisees over Jesus' command to "do as they say," and we have interpreted the term *hypocrites* to suit a (Protestant) Christian image of Judaism as a superficial religion of works-righteousness. Christians have legitimated vicious mistreatment of Jews by adducing Matthew's Gospel as a witness in favor of Christian bigotry, conversions under torture, pogroms, and—among some German Christians—the Holocaust itself. The mute witness of European Jewry's ashes impels some to the point of identifying Matthew's Gospel as an accomplice to genocide.

Yet even here the case for Matthew's anti-Judaism is not unambiguous. In the crucible of the Second World War, when the urgency of standing with or against Judaism was more pressing than it had been for centuries, Matthew's Gospel found a clear home in the camp of Judaism's defenders. Contrariwise, the German-Christian interpreters evidently felt that even the obvious condemnations of Pharisees, the demand for Jesus' blood, and the prophecies of persecution by synagogue leaders were of little propagandistic value when congregations would hear them in the context of the Sermon on the Mount's commendations of peacemakers and of love of enemies (and specifically persecutors). Though such theologians as Reichsbishop Ludwig Müller labored to produce a convincing Aryan version of the Sermon on the Mount, the political leadership and the propaganda officers were aware of an implacable opposition between Christianity and Nazism.[19] Even Müller's *"verdeutscht"* ("Germanized") presentation of Matthew seems directed at least as much against stirring up conflict among one's neighbors and against putting too high a value on attending church as it is against anything Jewish.[20] Müller even soft-pedals

Jesus' criticism of the Pharisees in Matthew 6:1ff.; whereas Matthew's Jesus advises that hypocritical *synagogue worshipers* love to trumpet their almsgiving in public, Müller's Jesus simply warns against hypocrisy in general.[21]

Conversely, those few who resisted National Socialism and defended European Jews enlisted Matthean texts as warrants for their actions. French Christian underground organizations such as the Cimade and Témoignage Chrétien undertook their risky operations in the name of God's "little ones," whom they felt obliged to help in Jesus' name.[22]

The Christians who risked their lives to shelter and rescue Jews in occupied France, the Netherlands, and Poland bought their copies of the New Testament from the same publishers that printed the collaborators' Bibles. They read aloud the same words from Matthew's Gospel and recognized the same cast of characters. The difference is not that the Chambonnais, for example, were poor interpreters and therefore missed the anti-Jewish ideology that ought to have impelled them to turn in their dangerous guests. The difference is that these righteous Gentile interpreters *didn't see the possibility* of an anti-Jewish interpretation of the Gospel of Matthew. They constituted a reading formation in which the relevant Matthean texts said, "Truly I tell you, just as you did it to one of the least of these of my family, you did it for me," not, "His blood be on us and on our children!" Consider the Chambonnais, noted in Susan Zuccotti's history for their commitment to those in need:

> Barot's and Poliakov's accounts both allude to the most important factor in the rescue success rate in Le Chambon—the determination of local residents to protect their guests. The people of Le Chambon lived in a state of constant alertness, with a warning system prepared. Their solidarity also made it difficult for potential informers to act. To whom could they safely leak information? Municipal authorities sympathized with the majority, as did, it appeared, many

of the police. Even local censors of mail were likely to prevent a denunciation. In such a situation, a careless informer might put himself in danger. In addition, it was psychologically more difficult for a solitary anti-Semite or opportunist to express his bile in a region where he was bucking an obvious majority.[23]

Conclusion

No one ought ever to minimize Christian responsibility in the abominable persecution of Jews over the centuries. But though we are obliged to acknowledge Christians' sins, we ought not let our commitment to honesty impel us to incautious conclusions regarding the reasons for atrocities against God's people of Israel. When we ascribe "anti-Judaism" to Matthew, we obscure several dimensions of the problem of bigotry. Matthew's Gospel is only one element in the reading formation that produces anti-Judaism—a reading formation of which we are all part.

It is far easier, however, to talk about Matthew's anti-Judaism than to examine our own ideological complicity with malign political forces. While contemporary critics adduce only the most laudable motives for lambasting Matthew, we ought to beware of blinding ourselves to more subtle effects of the ideology we hope to resist. The strength of Daniel Patte's searching essay on Matthean anti-Judaism is precisely his persistent willingness to examine his own unwilling role in perpetuating anti-Jewish readings of Paul and Matthew.[24] His non-anti-Jewish readings of these texts are provocative and persuasive. But even when we adopt Patte's positions, we have not extracted ourselves from the cultural conditions that made anti-Jewish readings possible and plausible in the first place.

The critical problem is not that the text of Matthew is anti-Jewish or that we as interpreters are anti-Jewish; the problem is that we live under conditions that make anti-Jewish readings too real and too attractive a possibility. Close readings of Matthew give legitimate grounds for the claim that Matthew's is a profoundly Judaic gospel. It upholds the validity of the law and insists on the authority of the Pharisees, it continues the Hebrew Bible's message of salvation to both Judeans and Gentiles, and it articulates the image of Israel's God in ways altogether familiar to readers of the Hebrew Bible. It even excoriates rival interpretations of true faith in ways that resemble the polemics of other Judaisms. The reason we find anti-Judaism in Matthew is that we live in a culture that has enacted just the sort of anti-Judaism we are claiming to discover.

The conclusion of this essay is not that Matthew is innocent of ideological error. Matthew may have been unacceptably antagonistic to certain varieties of Judaism, especially since we (in retrospect) see what Matthew could not see: much of what Matthew criticized in his contemporaries contributes to the continuing identity of Judaism. But if we want to redress the ideological wrongs done to Israel through centuries of hostile Christendom, our first obligation is not to spank Matthew for implanting anti-Jewish ideas in our heads; rather, we must live (converse, teach, interpret, preach) in ways that make anti-Judaism unthinkable.

Where we are willing to live without anti-Judaism, beyond bigotry and scapegoating altogether, there Matthew will never be thought an anti-Jewish text. Under such circumstances, interpreters not only will be able to read Matthew without an anti-Jewish "reading effect," but also will be in a position to embody and teach ways of life in which our neighbors can see our good works and glorify Israel's God in heaven.

CHAPTER FIVE

Integral and Differential Hermeneutics: The Significance of Interpretive Difference

The study of hermeneutics and the ethics of interpretation involve at least two leading questions. The first and more familiar is, How are we to understand texts? The second is, How shall we know whose interpretation is right (or true or legitimate)? Here I will describe this first approach as "integral" hermeneutics. The second, less familiar question challenges us to explain why the most knowledgeable and wisest interpreters so often disagree about what a text means. This approach I will characterize and advocate under the name "differential" hermeneutics.

Differential hermeneutics receives less vigorous attention in debates over meaning and interpretation. Essays in hermeneutics rarely address interpretive difference at all, and those that broach the topic typically elide the distinction between interpretive *difference* and interpretive *error*. If we instead made the study of interpretive difference a more prominent focus of hermeneutical discussion, we would be in a better position to characterize and weigh the differences among interpreters. Then we might acclimate ourselves to a hermeneutical ecology in which difference, far from implying error on one or another part, constitutes a positive contribution to a fuller understanding of textuality and (in the sphere of biblical interpretation) revelation. For these and other reasons, interpreters who care particularly about the convergence of ethics and interpretation ought to think twice before simply adopting a hermeneutic of "correctness" or "legitimacy." A hermeneutic that focuses on interpretive difference offers strengths that can mightily help interpreters make sense not only of the texts they study but also of the ways those texts inhabit and inform ethical and theological deliberation.

In the following summaries of integral and differential hermeneutics, I synthesize a variety of positions on each side. By synthesizing, I try in brief scope to articulate and interweave the leading characteristics of each position, but this allows the possibility, perhaps the likelihood, that my synthesis misrepresents the thought of the particular authors whom the summary covers. Readers should not for a moment mistake a heuristic overview for a detailed analysis of a particular scholar's thought. Still less should they suppose that if I identify weaknesses in a particular (summarized) approach, then each of the scholars whose work I summarize partakes equally in that weakness. Those interested in further examining these issues should turn to the specific works of the authors in question. I am a thoroughly interested party in the arguments over the merits of integral and differential hermeneutics. I have devoted considerable energy to articulating the case for differential hermeneutics, and I neither could nor would want to write an objective essay on the topic. This essay endeavors to sketch the terrain of the disagreement between integral and differential hermeneutics and to propose evaluations of the strengths and weaknesses of these two positions in the field in order to make clear the rationale for a differential hermeneutic.

The Integral Approach

The first of these lines of investigation—integral hermeneutics' search for a legitimate path to correct interpretation—has motivated most studies of hermeneutics. A moment's reflection reveals the reason that such studies often display a fervor that far outweighs their contribution to the debate over hermeneutics, a debate whose broad outlines have remained largely constant for decades. Once a scholar has figured out how to reach true understandings, he or she naturally feels disinclined to depart from that approach or even to entertain seriously the possibility of changing direction. Such a scholar may see colleagues who hesitate to adopt his or her newfound (or newly reaffirmed) true approach as recalcitrants who threaten the very structure of knowledge, the academy, even the church's teaching. To stave off such threats, scholars have long sought the definitive answer to the urgent question of how to interpret texts correctly. They have offered accounts of insight, understanding, empathy, intention, and various other features of legitimate hermeneutics. I call this search that emphasizes correct interpretation integral hermeneutics because it poses for itself (and for the domain of all meaning, over which it usually claims dominion) the task of articulating the positive characteristics of unitary interpretive truth.

Integral hermeneutics grounds its claim to preeminence on several premises. Some theories of integral hermeneutics posit a unique divinatory sympathy or understanding or meaning at which the interpreter must aim in order to qualify as methodologically legitimate. Some theorists, however, make an explicitly ethical defense of integral hermeneutics. This case—enunciated and elaborated by E. D. Hirsch[1]— maintains that textual interpretation by its very nature owes an ethical debt to the author's compositional intent. The author's intention equals the meaning of the text. Any interpretive deviation from attention to the author's intent counts as a (more or less valuable) "significance." Proponents of this interpretive ethic argue that readers should grant primary authority to interpretation that coheres with the author's intent as it took specific shape in the composition of the text (whether that author be construed as a human wordsmith or the Spirit who gives illumination and provocation to write). Because an author intended that we construe words in a single way, we as interpreters stand under an obligation to accede to the author's intent. Unless we acknowledge the determinative role of the author's compositional intent, we lack the criteria for distinguishing genuine meaning from counterfeit, exegesis from eisegesis, true divine teaching from hermeneutical legerdemain.

ARGUING THEIR CASE

The case for integral hermeneutics has developed into a finely nuanced complex of integrated arguments. While E. D. Hirsch presented the foundational work for this position in his studies in literary and philosophical hermeneutics, Anthony Thiselton, Francis Watson, and Kevin Vanhoozer stand as preeminent mediators of this approach to the field of biblical interpretation.[2] The cogency of their arguments has built upon a more generally held intuition that texts simply mean single things. These scholars have reinforced this beginning with sophisticated philosophical, theological, and ethical arguments on behalf of the premise that texts mean one thing: that which each text's author intended to mean. Their work has staked out and refined the integral approach, responding thoughtfully to any serious challenge to their enterprise. When opponents argue, for instance, that "the author's intention" is unsuitable as a criterion for assessing interpretations—perhaps it is unavailable or insufficiently distinct—the practitioners of integral hermeneutics respond by developing an account of their field that takes into consideration and overcomes their critics' objections by refining their conception of intentionality or defining more precisely their criteria of legitimate interpretation. Their conception of *how* to attain correct interpretation has shifted in response to challenges, but their impulse to attain the proper approach remains undeflected.

The philosophical case for integral hermeneutics proposes that meaning is a property of things called texts, so that "meaningless text" is a contradiction in terms. A text has a meaning built in; that meaning is the effect of the author's intentionality in composing the text. A text's meaning need not be obvious, although it can be. An octagonal red placard with the white letters *STOP* almost surely demands that approaching vehicles halt their forward motion at the point where it is located. But the meaning of a text such as Romans 7 has defied centuries of efforts to make it unambiguously clear. Nevertheless, Romans 7 does have a meaning; interpreters simply haven't yet arrived at a shared determination of that meaning with a degree of certainty that matches their certainty that octagonal red road signs require automobiles to stop. The text does not lack meaning, but interpreters lack agreement about what the meaning is.

According to these premises, a text's meaning subsists even though hidden, just as the back of a refrigerator continues to exist when no one observes it, or as the earthward side of a house's foundation continues to exist even when no one observes it (and when no one can state with certainty how far below the visible surface that earthward side lies or what it looks like). The presence of a cement floor in my basement provides sufficient evidence for me to infer the existence of its opposite side; the presence of a text in my hand provides sufficient evidence for me to infer the existence of its meaning. The intentional dimension of the text is its meaning, and when a text's meaning remains concealed, interpreters deploy a variety of devices to ascertain that hidden meaning.

The interpreter bears an ethical obligation to respect the authorial intention of the text because the meaning resides there. An interpreter who treats the text as though it means something other than its authorial intent distorts the truth about the text. Such interpretations are unjust to the author (who imbued the text with its meaning) and are capriciously inconsistent with the stability we expect of textual meaning in our everyday lives. A meaning inherent in texts demands our interpretive deference.

Moreover, a text exemplifies a type of communicative action: a meaningful action between an author and an auditor by means of a particular expression. The essence of communication rests on the premise that something controllable and specific is being conveyed from author to audience. If interpreters willfully ignore the author's communicative intent (while relying on their own readers to acknowledge *their* communicative intent), those interpreters transgress against the author and the reader both. Interpreters who flout the integrity of communicative action saw away the ethical limb on which they perch and undermine the deeply held human covenant that makes effective communication possible. An ethics of communicative action obligates all participants in the social bonds that permit communication to respect an author's communicative intent.

The tight integration that binds together participants in the communicative act and the text/meaning heightens the importance of the ethical question, How ought we to interpret texts? From the perspective of integral hermeneutics, the clear answer is that we should interpret texts in a way that expresses the meaning that constitutes the intentional dimension of the text as the author composed it. Likewise, we ought to interpret texts within the context of the author-text-audience configurations that inform them. To the extent that we treat texts (correctly, on this account) as communicative acts, we should observe the authorial and audience-oriented constraints at work on communication in order to find the perspective that correctly illuminates the meaning subsistent in the text, which connects the author and the audience.

Thus, the ethical case for integral hermeneutics rests to a great extent upon exegetical analyses of the natures of "text" and "communication." The advocates of this position find that neither the term *text* nor the notion of communication can sustain the possibility that texts do not possess the property of having a meaning. If texts lack this property, we lack the leverage necessary to account for the innumerable messages that humanity successfully composes and effectively responds to from moment to moment. The vast preponderance of clarity in communication testifies to the soundness of supposing that meaning subsists, somehow, in textuality.

CRITICIZING PLURALISM

The case for integral hermeneutics has dominated discussions of biblical hermeneutics in part because of this sophisticated reasoning that backs it up, but also partly because it tends to confirm a colloquial tendency to assume what should be demonstrated in this sort of argument. Common experience seems to confirm the premise that texts mean a single thing and that recipients of texts can usually determine that meaning with a high degree of confidence. So powerful is this intuition that detractors of integral hermeneutics have been reproached for performative contradiction if they endeavor to correct misapprehensions about their work. If an interpreter suggests that human communication admits of various interpretations but suggests that another critic has *mis*understood her work, she frequently encounters the charge that her own premise should allow others to interpret her work as they choose ("Now you're trying to say that there's only one correct way to understand your position!"). Some indeed have endured the less imaginative tactic of being told, "You have broccoli between your teeth," by a sly boots who thinks that one's impulse to check one's reflection in a mirror for stray vegetable matter "proves" that utterances have meanings as their property.

The debate over interpretation thus falls out with opponents to integral hermeneutics ostensibly holding up as a positive goal just exactly the interpretive wilderness that defenders of integral hermeneutics warn against. The principal counterposition to integral hermeneutics has typically been one or another mode of pluralism. While "pluralism" itself may stand for many different things, practitioners of integral hermeneutics have often represented pluralists as advocating divergence in interpretation as a positive value. A pluralist, on this account, would suppose that the more different interpretations one could devise, the better for all concerned. Moreover, a pluralist would have no particular ground on which to object to alleged misconstruals of his work.

Theorists of integral hermeneutics have (rightly) pointed out many philosophical, theological, and practical weaknesses of the pluralist case for meaning. Pluralism as a positive program for interpretation devolves rapidly into an uninteresting exercise in improbable, unsatisfying fancy. As long as pluralism (or "relativism") has stood as the only distinguishable alternative to integral hermeneutics, the integral program in hermeneutics has held center stage, especially with regard to interpretation of the Bible.

The Differential Approach

Recently, however, certain scholars have tried to outline a basis for a hermeneutics that begins from the ineluctable fact of interpretive difference. If, as a moment's perusal of the most respected journals of biblical scholarship will attest, the wisest and most careful interpreters have not been able to attain unanimity in ascertaining the meanings of the texts they examine, perhaps hermeneutics went wrong in supposing that "meaning" should be constrained to singularity, no matter how painstakingly defined or remotely deferred. Whereas recent interpretive discourses wrestle and bite to attain and hold preeminence over other approaches, in a former age—an era that modern scholars have dismissed as "precritical"—plurality in interpretation constituted a tolerable condition, indeed a positive dispensation from God. Augustine's *On Christian Doctrine* represents the sterling example of a theological celebration of plurality in interpretation (plurality that did not diminish the Scriptures' testimony to the one God of love and grace). Likewise, the varying traditions of spiritual exegesis affirm that readers might find an inexhaustible plenitude of quite legitimate interpretations of Scripture. When early Christian teachers criticize erroneous interpretations—as in Irenaeus famously saying that the Gnostics take the mosaic of a king and rearrange the pieces to form the picture of a dog—the argument doesn't insist on a single text-immanent meaning but relies

on what we might call a physiognomy of legitimate interpretation. Interpretations of Scripture that point toward the
Jesus whom the church recognizes in Scripture—that depict
the subject of the mosaic as a king, in other words—would
not fall under Irenaeus's anathema. The problem for Irenaeus is with interpretations that misrepresent Jesus, not
with a general plurality in interpretation.

Today's theorists of interpretative difference follow the
early church in not simply creating plurality as a good in and
of itself. Instead, they have begun putting together a way of
deliberating about hermeneutics that offers an explanation
for interpretive variety and complexes of criteria for evaluating better and worse interpretations. This hermeneutics
of difference does not resolve every interpretive problem
but offers ample advantages that may attract interpreters
dissatisfied with both pluralistic and integral hermeneutics.
A differential hermeneutic permits practitioners to see in
interpretive variety a sign of the variety in human imagination (in establishing historical facts as well as in drawing
theological inferences); to account positively for difference
among interpreters; to envision the practice of biblical interpretation less as a contest of experts and more as the shared
effort of Christian communities; and at the same time to
provide clearer, more specific, and more modest criteria for
correctness and legitimacy in interpretation.

The differential riposte to integral hermeneutics' ethical claim shifts attention away from interpreters' ethical
obligation to the author and toward their ethical obligation to their readers and one another. Instead of supposing that the nature of textuality involves a hermeneutical
trinity of author, text, and reader such that all readers must
strive to articulate an author's intentional meaning in the
text, practitioners of differential hermeneutics observe that
the act of offering an interpretation involves not only the
author and the text, but also one's interpretive colleagues
and the audience of the interpretation. Hence, interpreters
must devise interpretations that are accountable not only

to text and author, but also to rival interpreters and audiences. Moreover, the divided churches have sought justification for their sides of various ecclesiastical disputes by appealing to Scripture, yet this tactic loses much of its force if one allows that Scripture may also offer support for the opposite party's opinion. The integral-hermeneutic quest for single textual meaning feeds on, and in turn itself feeds, theological conflicts. Finally, integral hermeneutics benefits from its advocates having made their premises so familiar that any alternative approach to interpretation must either justify itself on terms indigenous to integral hermeneutics (terms that strongly favor the outlook that generates them) or suffer the dubiety that accompanies the impression that the alternative hermeneutic neglects apparently necessary aspects of hermeneutical reasoning. Familiarity with a dominant point of view breeds contempt for alternative ways of considering an issue.

One God, One Right Interpretation?

Integral hermeneutics derives further strength from theological buttresses to its philosophical ramparts. Inasmuch as God is one and God's will cannot err or equivocate ("For God is a God not of disorder but of peace," as the apostle Paul said in 1 Cor. 14:33), so the written communication of God's word must not permit ambiguity in expression or plurality in interpretation. God's will is perfectly expressed in the words of Scripture. Interpreters therefore stand under the obligation to seek and promulgate that singular divine intent. Likewise, the communicative triad of author, text, and reader matches the theological Trinity of Father, Son, and Spirit. Finally, many scholars identify the necessity of interpretation with the fall from grace in Eden. The prelapsarian humans enjoyed unambiguous, "uninterpreted" converse with one another and with God. Since interpretation manifests itself as a consequence of sinful rebellion, faithful readers should strive for the true meaning as they strive to resist sin. The congruence of God's unitary purpose and triune identity with the text's (alleged) singular meaning and triadic appropriation, along with the apparent sinfulness of multiplicity in interpretation, reinforces the integral-hermeneutic case for singularity in meaning and for the obligation to aim for that meaning in our encounter with texts.[3]

All these reasons combine to give integral hermeneutics the high ground in debates over interpretation. The case for the alternative, differential hermeneutics, rests on reasoning every bit as sophisticated as that for integral hermeneutics, but the differential side lacks the support of conventional wisdom and ecclesiastical approval. Its force depends on readers stepping outside what they have taken for granted about hermeneutics and considering the hermeneutical problem differently from the start. Because familiarity does not by itself constitute an argument in support of integral hermeneutics, the unfamiliarity of alternative approaches to hermeneutics should not count against the case their proponents argue.

PERSISTENT DIFFERENCES

A practitioner of differential hermeneutics does not begin by wondering what the correct interpretive method (or approach or perspective) might be or even by assuming that the question itself makes sense. Differential hermeneutics arises from the observation that people interpret constantly and so successfully that they manage extremely complex lives in indifferent, even hostile social environments. On the whole, people seem remarkably skillful at interpretation. The proponents of integral hermeneutics should welcome this aptitude; it tends to underscore the weight of their argument from communicative action. But at this point the differential interpreter raises this frustrating question: Why do the most erudite, pious, intelligent, and expert interpreters of Scripture so rarely agree with one another?

This ubiquity of interpretive difference motivates a heterogeneous scattering of scholars—Daniel Patte, Charles Cosgrove, James K. A. Smith, Stephen Fowl, myself, and perhaps the most recent work of Elisabeth Schüssler Fiorenza as well, among others[4]—to press ethical questions that concern not just the author and the text alone. Instead, the differential interpreters ask how we can account for the differences among rivals' interpretations, especially when those interpreters show all the signs of extraordinary intelligence, wide and deep acquaintance with relevant historical and literary context, and even genuine reverence for the subjects of the texts in question.

Consider more closely this blind spot of integral hermeneutics. When Hans Dieter Betz, Donald Carson, and Amy-Jill Levine interpret the Sermon on the Mount, they bring to bear all the capacities of spirit and intellect to which a biblical interpreter might aspire.[5] Even so, their interpretations of that text diverge in numerous important ways. By the theory of integral hermeneutics, only one of them has truly interpreted the sermon; the other two propound more or less gravely erroneous interpretations (unless all three have gone astray!). This state of affairs constitutes a troubling ramification for integral hermeneutics, since we who have not attained to the foremost ranks of biblical interpretation must try to discern which of these three interpreters offers the soundest interpretation. Moreover, we do so without the full extent of the knowledge that each of these interpretive leaders brings to bear (else we would stand with them at the cutting edge). We must decide which of the three has correctly interpreted Matthew's Gospel, but we lack the scholarly standing requisite to adjudicate the question. If even these three leading scholars disagree, we would need to know more than they do in order to make an authoritative decision for or against their positions. But under the circumstances, we do not know even as much as they do; still less do we possess the deeper understanding that would enable us to determine on which scholar we should rely.

RESPECTFUL DISSENT

More troubling still, a proponent of integral hermeneutics can in the end offer no respectful account of why anyone would disagree with him or her. The most honorable explicit explanation of difference under the integral approach runs more or less as follows: "She doesn't understand the text [or the history or the culture or the background influences] as well as I do." We mask such pretensions with claims such as, "He does not take full account of . . .," or "He doesn't show acquaintance with . . .," or "He doesn't consider . . . ," or "She accords inappropriate weight to this and insufficient attention to that." But these expressions all amount to claiming that *I* have the soundest insight into this text and all others have fallen short in one way or another.

Sometimes interpreters offer less charitable explanations of interpretive difference. We sometimes describe others' divergence from our conclusions in terms of their having succumbed to inappropriate influences. They are fundamentalists or radical skeptics or feminists or patriarchs or racists or "politically correct" or traditionalists or victims of brainwashing by the dominant cultural environment. (Thanks be to God that we, or perhaps just I, have escaped such pernicious influences!) Sometimes we chalk up divergence to ignorance or moral weakness—a desire for publicity or approval, let us say, or financial greed, or the hunger for a biblical rationale for indulging other unspiritual appetites. Explanations such as these fit the assumptions of integral hermeneutics perfectly but leave other pivotal questions unanswered. How did one scholar avoid the subtle pitfalls that so confound others? Does a reader who is interpreting under the influence of something bad know that he or she is beclouded, and if not, how can we be sure that interpreters who vigorously proclaim their innocence of ideological determination are not simply unconscious of the deeper influences bearing down on them?

At the end of a debate conducted under the auspices of integral hermeneutics, one is left only with the alternatives of saying that one's rival is ignorant, less intelligent, misguided, perverse, or insane. If she knew the relevant factors as well as the correct interpreter—you or me—and if she understood the proper weight to ascribe to each bit of evidence, she, too, would assent to our interpretation. At the most polite, one can decline to speculate as to why one's rival disagrees; in more candid moments, practitioners allow that their interlocutors simply work with their vision narrowed by commitments that the (correct) interpreter doesn't hold. Yet without a strong account of how it is that wise, learned interpreters come to disagree with one another, a theory of how *correctly* to understand a text risks serving flatly as a justification for one interpretive party's efforts to shout louder than all others. Each participant in an interpretive disagreement arrives at the point of dissent by way of confidence that he or she has pursued the correct understanding with a legitimate method. That which an advocate of integral hermeneutics proposes as a diligent effort to ascertain the true meaning of the text, a supporter of differential hermeneutics may see as a mystified expression of an interpretive will to power—an example of what Elisabeth Schüssler Fiorenza might diagnose as "kyriarchy," the unholy union of power-over with spiritual leadership.[6]

In contrast, on the account of differential hermeneutics, the explanations for interpretive difference proliferate. These by no means exclude ignorance, intellectual limitation, error, perversity, or madness, but they include positive characteristics as well. The differential interpreter can frankly admit that presuppositions make knowledge possible but also limit knowledge, such that our capacity to sympathize with ancient perspectives on the nature of reality may, for instance, inhibit our capacity to note and acknowledge our complicity with contemporary oppressive political forces. Or, to give another example, our profound acquaintance with recent scholarship on postcolonialism and subaltern literature may overshadow our attention to the grammatical nuances of the text. Most scholars have observed some of their colleagues riding interpretive hobbyhorses, solving every exegetical conundrum with a single interpretive device, whether it be chiasm, honor/shame dynamics, deconstruction, reader-response criticism, etymology, or whatever. Pertinent though these all may be to interpretive discernment, it is doubtful that any one of them resolves every dilemma. To a less obvious degree, all interpreters favor a particular limited range of exegetical explanations and depreciate others. Just as the hobbyhorse jockey may be faulted for employing too limited a range of interpretive tools, so we all may advocate a range of interpretive preferences that, while generally sound, undervalues contributions from the fields we do not ourselves prefer. In short, differential hermeneutics begins with the recognition that different interpreters have good reasons for adopting different interpretations, reasons that cannot be exhaustively or even thoroughly evaluated. The criteria by which we evaluate our rationales are themselves, after all, subject to evaluation—and so on to an infinite regress.

Proponents of integral hermeneutics are liable to respond quickly that on this account of differential hermeneutics, no interpretation can be better than another, or that differential hermeneutics renders all interpretive decisions radically subjective. They collapse differential hermeneutics into a purely pluralistic hermeneutic in which all interpretations are merely interpretations, none better than another, with no reason to adopt one rather than another. One can offer an immediate practical rebuttal to this objection by observing, once again, that practitioners of differential approaches simply do not behave or argue as this objection presumes. At this point, most proponents of integral hermeneutics insist that differential interpreters must be pluralists or that they have no reason for approving one interpretation rather than another. On the premises of integral hermeneutics, this may be true, but the practitioners of differential hermeneutics do not assent to the premises of integral hermeneutics.

Criteria for Validity

Differential hermeneutics proceeds by identifying the criteria by which an interpretation claims validity, the soundness of that claim, and the scope of that claim and those criteria. All criteria, on this account, are local criteria. Some criteria are narrowly local. As particular schools of biblical interpretation exemplify, an interpretation that would be warmly received at Harvard might reasonably and appropriately be less welcome at Fuller, and vice versa. Other criteria extend to groups so expansive as to seem universal, although in such cases one should remember that the term *universal* includes many more interpreters than "everyone I can think of," however often confident interpreters ignore this fact. The claim that a premise holds universally can be disconfirmed, after all, if a single interpreter dissents.

Interpretive agreement indicates not the discovery of a hitherto-concealed "true meaning" but the convergence of interpreters' priorities and sensibilities, such that two interpreters share a sense of which aspects of the text count and how to associate the pertinent aspects of the text with cultural, grammatical, theological, and other such correlates in the broader communicative environment. Agreement arises most readily among readers who learned about the Bible from the same teachers, who share interests, whose theologies (or lack thereof) converge, and so on. Such convergence doesn't dissolve agreement into congruent formation, as though identical (academic, theological) twins would automatically agree on interpretive issues simply because of their training. One need not look far to find examples of classmates and denominational colleagues who disagree bitterly with one another. When readers agree, however, they attest a common evaluation of a variety of dimensions of interpretation. These common evaluations are more likely when readers inhabit common educational and theological spheres.

Moreover, the local criteria that derive from identity and experience intersect, envelop, and overlap each other. My outlook on interpretation has been informed by my adherence to Anglican ecclesial identity and to the catholic wing of that expansive communion. But my interpretations have likewise been formed by the institutions at which I have studied (and taught), by writings of and friendships with scholars at schools where I have not studied, by my upbringing in a home redolent of respect for the English literary canon (especially Shakespeare and the English novel), by my undergraduate philosophy major, by my ministries in inner-city parishes, by my familiarity with a variety of languages, by my participation in ministries to people affected with AIDS, and so on indefinitely. No single set of interpretive priorities always takes precedence over all others, although my perspective shows enough consistency that readers who are well acquainted with my work can suggest that such-and-such an interpretation is predictable or that another is surprising. In other words, although no single criterion (or set of criteria) determines a particular interpreter's perspective on a text, the problem of assessing interpretations derives not from the paucity of available criteria but from the superabundance of possible criteria.

One can legitimately criticize my postmodern predilections, for instance, on the basis that my whole entanglement with postmodern theory is misguided and dangerous from the outset, or that I do not understand the scholars whom I pretend to draw on, or that my postmodern premises (although neither intrinsically misguided not misconstrued) are simply wrong. If I make a technical argument that the history of first-century Judaism, the grammar and rhetoric of the ancient texts, and the canons of historical plausibility that predominate among the practitioners of historical reasoning in the major academies of Europe and North America all support my claim that Jesus of Nazareth most closely resembles a wandering Jewish Cynic-like figure, then the bounds of my argument's authority extend just as far as my audience assents to my premises. Somebody who dissents from Euro-American scholarly norms or who cares not a bit about first-century Judaism or who relies on the King James Version of the Bible may not be interested in my argument. (We can argue about whether such a person *should* demur from my priorities, but for now, granted the possibility of such a person's existence, we will allow him or her these predispositions.) Differential hermeneutics does not banish judgments about correctness but ties these judgments to specific premises that constitute the particular interpretive process.

Whereas integral hermeneutics falters over the question of whence disagreements arise, differential hermeneutics abounds with possible reasons for adopting one interpretation rather than another. A differential hermeneutic can stipulate explicitly what counts as a good reason within a particular interpretive discourse, without demanding that every interpretive discourse adhere to that criterion. Thus, African-American hermeneutics will produce interpretations that vary from those produced under hermeneutical approaches that do not attend specifically to racial contingencies. Literary-critical interpreters will advance exegetical results that derive their cogency not necessarily from attention to the historical background of the text in question but from observations about the interplays of character, plot, diction, and so on (which may themselves interweave, to varying degrees, with historical discourses). Anglican interpreters will, with sound reason, propose interpretations that differ from those offered by Southern Baptist interpreters—not because of a pernicious influence that clouds the minds of theologically motivated interpreters, but precisely because the cast of mind that inspires one to sympathize with the Southern Baptist tradition may incline one to weigh interpretive decisions differently from one's Anglican colleagues. Scholars who adhere to no particular ecclesiastical tradition are not thereby uninfluenced, but are influenced by a different array of ideals. Were such denominational, philosophical, or cultural alliances subject to disinterested comparison and criticism, one might attain to an intellectual clarity that permitted the sort of judgment that integral hermeneutics requires; under the conditions

of mortal knowledge, however, advocacy of integral hermeneutics amounts to a kind of interpretive ethnocentrism.

Diversity: As in Creation, So in Interpretation

From the perspective of differential hermeneutics, the limitations of human understanding and interpretation do not
derive from sin and the fall but, like diversity in human
constitution and identity, signal the human distinction from
God and serve to give God glory precisely by the harmonious expression of their difference. As parts of the body
are not all eyes, feet, hands, or nose, so interpretations of
Scripture are not all historically warranted assertions about
the original intent of a human (or divine) author, nor is
interpretive differentiation any more a result of sin than is
corporal differentiation. Again, the very existence of difference serves the positive purpose of enabling human beings,
whose individual limitations cannot satisfactorily represent
God, to begin to represent truth by the harmonious ordering of differentiated bodies and interpretations.

Similarly, the claim that the interpretive triad of author,
text, and reader reflects God's triune identity as a sort of
literary *vestigium trinitatis* (vestige of the Trinity) fails to
account for the possibility that the constitutive elements
of interpretation number some quantity other than three.
Perhaps context also should be reckoned among the characteristics of the interpretive situation. Indeed, the author's
context and the reader's context may both make fair claims
to stand among the definitive elements of an interpretive
act. Moreover, numbers other than three carry theological
significance within the Christian tradition. Four might be
a more appropriate number for theological constituents of
interpretive practice, since four Gospels interpret the identity of Jesus to his disciples. Without multiplying examples
indefinitely, the argument from triunity should be granted
ornamental, not probative, force.

Last, although God's will is perfect, singular, and uncon-fused, our appropriation of these terms should attend to the likelihood that these attributes function differently with regard to God's intentions than with regard to ours, with regard to God's thoughts than with regard to our thoughts. While we might assent to the proper unity of God's literary intent in inspiring Scripture, could we but see with God's eyes, we ought not simply assume that singularity in human interpretation reflects fittingly the complex unity of God's purpose. Integral hermeneutics provides one coherent way of positing a connection between meaning, interpretation, divine identity, and the Christian theological tradition; dif-ferential hermeneutics proposes another coherent approach to connecting these dots and does so without some of the problematic implications of integral hermeneutics.

The extent to which local cultural currents determine interpretation, for example, motivates some proponents of differential hermeneutics to pay particular attention to interpretive discourses in Africa, Asia, Latin America, and among indigenous peoples, discourses to which the domi-nant European and North American schools typically pay only cursory attention, when they attend at all. Proponents of integral hermeneutics certainly do not cultivate a delib-erate policy of excluding interlocutors based on race or culture, but when they interact only with interpretations from other Euro-American interpreters (or with interpret-ers from outside Europe and North America only to the extent that those interpreters reflect Euro-American criti-cal priorities), they effect a culturally colored exclusion, whether deliberately or inadvertently. Moreover, since inte-gral hermeneutics allows for only a single standard of legiti-macy, if a practitioner of integral hermeneutics excludes any particular groups of interpreters, that exclusion implies the group's lack of legitimate interpretive authority.

Differential hermeneutics, in contrast, describes inter-pretive practices as always necessarily imbued with cultural specificity, such that Euro-American interpreters would not ordinarily be expected to interact with interpreters from non-Western cultures. If Euro-American interpreters do scan more distant cultural horizons, they may legitimately do so without justifying their research as seeking the correct interpretation, seeking instead to learn critically from readers whose angle of vision enables them to see texts in ways excluded by customary Western approaches. Differential interpreters may pursue such illumination in the name of inclusivity or of liberation from theology's Constantinian captivity of Western culture. Or they may do so out of their humble appreciation that interpretive wisdom dwells with interpreters lacking academic training as well as with those who hold advanced degrees, with inhabitants of any continent, indeed with illiterate as well as erudite readers, recalling Jesus' prayer, "I thank you, Father, Lord of heaven and earth, because you have hidden these things from the wise and the intelligent and have revealed them to infants; yes, Father, for such was your gracious will" (Matt. 11:25–26).

That humility does not necessitate a romantic inerrancy-of-the-primitive. One can assess nonacademic readings critically without either dismissing them for failure to meet the local standards of twenty-first-century Northern, Western culture or abjectly deferring to the privilege of a romanticized outsider. For critically evaluating nonacademic (or non-Western or nonhistorical) readings, however, one should learn to recognize nonacademic criteria without prejudging them as "precritical" or naïve. Interpreters from all times and places exercise critical judgment and will always critically appraise interpretations from other contexts. A richly critical, ethical, theologically sound practice of interpretive discernment will develop the capacity to distinguish stronger from weaker interpretations by a variety of different sets of criteria.

The geocultural aspect of differential hermeneutics entails momentous implications for missional theology. Past generations of evangelists and expositors have often sought to inculcate an authoritative version of integral hermeneutics along with inviting their neighbors to share in the welcoming grace of God. On their assumptions, the unity of the presence of Christ, made manifest in the singular meaning of the text, requires learning not only the stories, the laws, and the wisdom and counsel of Scripture but also the authorized mode for interpreting. If the presence of Christ abides not in the "letter," however, but in the Spirit who integrates separated people and nations into one body, then a differential hermeneutic may more fitly acknowledge the Spirit's freedom to make the meaning of Scripture active in various peoples in various ways.

Conclusion

Differential hermeneutics provides a way of thinking about correct interpretation that respects the relevance of particular criteria and the necessity of attending to the applicable criteria at all times and in all places. A practitioner of differential hermeneutics can comfortably uphold some interpretations as right and reject others as wrong without self-contradiction. Since criteria and contexts always infuse interpretation, interpreters will always encounter canons by which critics distinguish better from worse interpretations. At the same time, differential hermeneutics does not extrapolate from the criteria that one critic applies in one situation to a universal set of norms for distinguishing valid from invalid interpretations. Integral hermeneutics practically implies ongoing interpretive conflict among Christians. What, shall we wonder, is the single correct meaning of, for example, Jesus' blessing of Simon Peter in Matthew 16:18, the prohibition of a woman having "authority over a man" in 1 Timothy 2:12, the New Testament descriptions of baptism, the genocidal wars of God in the conquest narratives? Differential hermeneutics, by contrast, recognizes that disciples will always adopt divergent interpretations of the Bible (and of their life-worlds as well), so that the unity by which believers bespeak their allegiance to the one God derives not from their consensus about the textual meaning of Scripture but from the obligation to bear with one another, to testify to the truth as we have received it, and to continue to show forbearance and patience in the shared hope that when all things are revealed, the Revealer will also display the manner in which our diverse interpretations form a comprehensive concord in ways that now elude our comprehension.

In expressing such a hope, this advocate of differential hermeneutics draws near again, I think, to the proponents of integral hermeneutics. The advocates of integral hermeneutics do not, after all, deny the existence of varying interpretations, nor do they repudiate faith in a wisdom greater than human interpretive insight. As readers who operate under the sign of differential hermeneutics can stoutly argue for the correctness of a particular interpretation, so readers who adhere to the premises of integral hermeneutics can allow that no mortal interpretation will attain finality and that advocates of various competing interpretive claims can each usually cite a cornucopia of reasons in defense of their respective interpretations.

The operative distinction between differential and integral hermeneutics involves a particular sort of ethical argument. In this case, the ethical question concerns not so much "Who's right and who's wrong?" as "What sort of lives and interactions should our hermeneutics engender?" The integral quest for rectitude and unity bespeaks the unique identity and perfect will of God but with the consequence of setting readers over against one another in an interpretive contest without end. The differential vision of hermeneutics leaves final answers to the questions of rectitude and unity in God's hands, and espouses instead the shared endeavor of patiently and respectfully cultivating distinct, concordant testimonies to God's glory, from every tribe and language and people and nation.

CHAPTER SIX
Walk This Way:
Repetition, Difference,
and the Imitation of Christ

By now, the "What Would Jesus Do?" craze has probably peaked. Savvy entrepreneurs have saturated the Christian youth market with bracelets, earrings, and some other outlandish things. Though five-color silk-screened T-shirts will continue to sell well, the boom in WWJD paraphernalia has settled into a steadier, more modest array of commercial possibilities.

Of course, WWJD resurrects a long-standing tradition. The classic in this genre is Thomas à Kempis's *The Imitation of Christ*; more recently, Charles Sheldon captured the imaginations of millions with *In His Steps*, the best-selling novel that challenged turn-of-the-twentieth-century Christians to follow Jesus more nearly. Indeed, my copy of *In His Steps* bears on its dust jacket the subtitle *What Would Jesus Do?*[1] Such theological commodities as WWJD bracelets, Brethren spiritual direction, and novelistic exhortations attract large, enthusiastic commercial attention. Indeed, these antimaterialist tracts conventionally make much of their popularity; the foreword of *In His Steps* notes boastfully that the English edition itself sold three million copies, and *The Imitation of Christ* is often alleged to have sold more copies than any book other than the Bible itself.[2]

No one need squander much time debunking the superficial nonethics of "What Would Jesus Do?" trinkets; one is tempted to think of Jesus' own peremptory response to the merchants in the temple. Yet interest in an ethics based on the imitation of Christ persists, and the premise demands critical attention, particularly in light of the frequent scriptural commands to do what Jesus does and Paul's exhortation to imitate him (as he himself imitates Christ). Is an imitation-ethic in any way legitimate, or are all of our endeavors to align our lives with those of Jesus and Paul fundamentally misguided?

A Critique of Imitation-Ethics

One may object in the first instance that imitation-ethics rests on a category mistake. Since Jesus' role in salvation history is unique, we may conclude that we ought no more to take Jesus, or even the apostle Paul, as our model of behavior than we ought to presume to build a tower that reaches to heaven.

Whereas this time-honored distinction of theological roles resists imitation-ethics on the grounds that it goes too far across boundaries that should rather be sternly enforced (for everyone's well-being), another basis for criticizing an imitation-ethic might lie in the possibility that the "imitation" of Christ does not go far enough. Michael Cartwright, for one, argues that imitation is not an adequate basis for discipleship—at least, not imitation in the Sheldonian sense.[3] Though the characters in *In His Steps* ostensibly endeavor to imitate Christ in their daily lives, Cartwright notes that this novel evades the kind of radical discipleship that would rock established power structures (in society in general and in the church itself). The characters do not immediately forsake privilege and adopt itinerant apostleship. Rather, they *take a pledge*—a noncompulsory work of what one might call supererogation if the characters and setting weren't flagrantly Protestant—a one-year experimental pledge to ask themselves what Jesus would do.

Cartwright underlines an underlying pathos to the Sheldonian quest. The pledge that characters take is voluntary;[4] Pastor Henry Maxwell doesn't propose that walking in Jesus' steps be *expected* of his congregation. Moreover, the content of Sheldonian imitation is problematic. Maxwell and his friends, anticipating modern conundrums over the temporal abyss that separates "what it meant" from "what it means," confess that they know of no clear answer to the question they have volunteered to ask. Jesus' and Paul's specific teachings are evidently obscure to the First Church disciples.[5] Where Scripture and the millennia of Christian practice overflow with concrete examples of what Jesus would do, Sheldon invites us to supererogatory fantasizing about what we *might* do. Finally, the pervasive individualism that forms an unquestioned dimension of Sheldon's new discipleship— an individualism in which each believer is accountable only to God by way of the Holy Spirit—diverges sharply from a biblical emphasis on communal solidarity, an emphasis that might go a long way toward alleviating the vacuity that haunts First Church's discipleship.

In short, Sheldon and his surrogate, Pastor Maxwell, sponsor not a true "new discipleship," but a pallid, remote, attenuated good-fellowship. He demonstrates a sort of inverse square law of discipleship, whereby a presupposed distance from Jesus generates an ethos that is geometrically less arresting than the apostolic preaching: Sheldon's brand of ethics will neither stand close comparison to the teaching of Jesus nor make any unwelcome claim on the lives of modern churchgoers.

Imitation-ethics provokes criticism from yet another angle. Elizabeth Castelli calls into question the ideological-political dimension of Paul's ethics; her monograph *Imitating Paul* analyzes the familiar Pauline mimesis motif from the perspective of Michel Foucault's writings on power and social relations. This theoretical starting point enables Castelli to trace the dangerous manifestation of "one particularly poignant sign of the more general drive toward singularity, sameness, and truth in much Christian discourse,"[6] where others have seen nothing more threatening than an elementary pedagogical tactic. According to Castelli's Foucauldian reading, Paul invoked the language of imitation as a power-full weapon to ward off the unfettered diversity that threatened Paul's understanding of the gospel.

Castelli identifies the most relevant aspect of Foucault's discourse on power as his sketch of "pastoral power," a novel twist on the personal ethics that early Christianity introduced into its Hellenistic environment.[7] The most familiar ancient social formations marshaled power to shore up the pyramid of terrestrial dominion. Pastoral power, however, orders the lives of individuals (as well as communities) so as to ensure the heavenly well-being of all. Pastoral power functioned by appealing to the souls of believers, knitting each to all, subordinating any single believer's well-being to the interests of the whole community while at the same time addressing itself to the individual's own conscience. Pastoral power renounces imperial coercion for the more insidious compulsion of the haunted conscience.

Castelli notes a pattern in Paul's use of the imitation motif in 1 Thessalonians 1:6 and 2:14; Philippians 3:17; and 1 Corinthians 4:16 and 11:1, which urge readers to "be imitators of me."[8] Where Paul confronts dissension, he demands that his congregations be more like him—establishing himself as the norm of Christian behavior, denying the value of diversity of belief and practice in Christian communities, and articulating the principle that "Christians are Christians insofar as they strive for the privileged goal of sameness."[9]

Not only does Castelli show a Paul who precipitates an economy of homogeneity in early Christianity, she also traces the ways Paul's rhetoric enters and defines the institutional texture of the church. Though (as she recognizes) the organizational structure of the church remains fluid long after Paul's death, yet his ideology of pastoral power prolonged a hierarchical sensibility in which "submission" (of stronger to weaker, of believers to their leaders, of wives to husbands, of slaves to their masters, of children to parents) coalesced as the currency of Christian virtue. The passivity of Paul's imitation-formula "Be imitators of me" betokens the passivity that Paul imparts to believers as their appropriate way of life.

These two profoundly distinct lines of resistance to imitation-ethics give ample reason for a casual reader to suppose that the whole enterprise amounts only to wan simulation and pernicious subordination. Add to these the commonplace critique that the "imitation of Jesus" confuses the distinct character of the unique Savior of humankind with our own radically flawed personae, and the case for an imitation-ethic may seem a dead letter.

What Would Jesus Have Us Do?

All the same, the question of what Jesus would do, what Jesus would say, is in some sense inescapable for Christians. One would be hard-pressed to imagine a Christian *way* that disposed of Jesus' attitudes and teachings.[10] What would be left? Yet if some kind of continuity with Jesus is necessary to Christianity, while the "imitation of Christ" entails critical pitfalls, whither shall earnest, diligent, thoughtful Christians turn for guidance?

After Castelli's Foucauldian critique of Paul and his rhetoric of imitation, one might be inclined to think postmodern theory the *least* likely resource for discerning a positive value in the ethics of imitation. Still, postmodern theoreticians frequently remind their readers that no cultural formation is intrinsically benign or malign. That drug which is poison in some circumstances is medicine in another. The postmodern critique of identity and homogeneity that impels Castelli to raise caution flags along the Pauline way can provide subsequent interpreters with a way to imagine their perpetuation of Jesus' example, and Paul's.

The force of Castelli's warning concerns the danger, observable in the church's behavior throughout history, of construing "imitation" as the working out of a hierarchical drive toward Sameness, and at the same time as the construction of a dangerous Other (the heathen, the Jew, the witch, the primitive native, the freethinker, and always the heretic). The point is demonstrably well taken, but much remains to be said about this premise, on a variety of fronts. The postmodern fascination with identity and difference—or "alterity"—ramifies further than a casual reader of Castelli might suppose. A thoughtful appropriation of particular strands of postmodern thought offers the promise of a mode of discipleship that acknowledges the theological-ethical value of an imitation-ethic while avoiding the trap of constituting one particular instantiation of identity as normative for participants in the Christian tradition.[11]

Postmodern theorists have demonstrated a multifaceted fascination with the question of identity. Indeed, to oversimplify to an extreme, one might define the postmodern as the suspicion of "identity." To unpack that claim: One characteristic of modern thought concerns an imperative to discover identity, in the sense of "things that are the same," wherever possible. Modern thought, on this count, is the acme of an Aristotelian logic that assumes that A and not-A cannot simultaneously be true. Postmodern thought follows the Heraclitean path and observes that A itself is never *simply* "the same" from one moment to the next (or in any two places). How much less can we suggest that A and B might somehow be called "the same," unless we willfully suppress awareness of their differences?

From this interrogation of the entire notion of identity, a postmodern theorist may develop any number of tactics for revisiting modern discourses and deflecting them from the directions that seem obvious, natural, and necessary to a modernity that takes identity for granted. This chapter, for example, concerns the legitimacy of an ethics of imitation (the imitation of Christ, Paul's exhortation to "be imitators of me," and even WWJD). I will therefore walk with readers through several postmodern explorations of identity and difference, imitation and repetition before we return to ponder the role of these motifs in Christian discipleship.

Identity and Difference

Much of the Western philosophical tradition has simply taken the phenomenon of identity for granted. In the complications that unreel as one examines life closely, thinkers have sought underlying patterns of sameness, setting "identity" as the foundation stone of their systems. In so doing, they have opted for the Eleatic path to knowledge, some degree of an investment in the changelessness of Being. True arguments and judgments, on this account, depend on their universality; one tries to reason from undeniable claims. This mode of reasoning presupposes that one can treat objects that share particular properties as identical (with regard to those properties), and in Aristotle's words, "It is impossible for the same attribute at once to belong and not to belong to the same thing and in the same relation."[12] The principle of noncontradiction buttresses Aristotle's distinction between essence and accident, by which he isolates the primordial basis of identity. Such reasoning stakes pivotal importance to "sameness" without subjecting the logic of identity to sufficient scrutiny. Indeed, Aristotle tries to fend off scrutiny of the legitimacy of his principle by arguing that anyone who would ask for proof of the law of noncontradiction demonstrates *apaideusia*—a lovely choice of words that connotes ignorance, lack of education, boorishness, and bad form. The philosophical tradition has perpetuated Aristotle's willingness to posit this as the most certain of all principles, one that cannot be doubted. Yet Aristotle grounds this undoubtable certainty in a mere gesture of exclusion, marking off those who are willing to examine the principle of noncontradiction.

What happens when one looks closely at the principle of identity? One faces the conundrum that wherever one searches for identity, one encounters difference, such that one must introduce limiting clauses to focus an alleged sameness on a distinct range of qualities. Take two white plastic coffee cups printed with the emblem of the Episcopal Diocese of Maine. The first plastic coffee cup may be the same as the next one in its composition, dimensions, and markings, but it was injection-molded at a different time and does not occupy the same physical location. Even the qualities I have just stipulated to be identical often diverge. Though the shapes of the two cups may *appear* identical, one may have been subjected to heat and stress that have rendered it slightly ovoid, while its neighbor retains a perfect circularity. The evenness of the coloration will probably vary between the two cups. We may safely treat the two cups as identical only so long as someone does not (boorishly) press too hard beyond appearances. At every point, though, judgments of sameness and difference derive from particular larger contexts with reference to which observers will construe some similarities as establishing identity or some divergences as constituting difference.

The arch-interrogator of identity was Heraclitus, who notoriously taught that one cannot step into the same river twice. When one tries to step in the second time, the river has changed; it is no longer simply "the same."[13] Though the point may seem trivial, it undermines the "obvious" and "natural" character of Aristotle's presumption of identity. Even the firmest advocates of the importance of identity will acknowledge that terms such as *the same* must be used with reference to specific qualities; we can always find *some* differences between two items. Thus, if in conversation someone asks whether Frank and I drive the same car, hearers customarily construe the inquiry as a question about brands and models, not joint ownership. If the question were about joint ownership, one might offer an annoying but accurate Heraclitean answer by saying, "No, when he drives, the odometer reading is always different from when I drive" (one can never step into the same Riviera twice).

Much of modern discourse leans heavily on the principle of identity. Identity funds not only the arguments of modernity, but even the social, economic, and educational dimensions of modernity. Jean-François Lyotard proposes that the modern condition places the highest value on "performativity" and orients its agencies toward efficiency, productivity, and growth.[14] Systems, however, buy efficiency and productivity at the cost of attention to detail. Most readers of this book will have experienced the dislocation that arises when one is treated simply as a member of a particular generic set, whether it be as the "Occupant" of junk mail, or as the undifferentiated "Christian" whom popular media often depict as credulous and hypocritical, or as the normative white male of the dominant cultural scene. This sort of dislocation is especially sharp if one does not conform to the assumed stereotype of the set, but is no less eerie even if the shoe fits perfectly. We long to feel as though each of us is different in significant ways from the rest, but the devices of modern marketing will find a way to categorize us, the better to sell us sneakers. Ironically, the modern defenders of identity will claim that they are defending individuality and identity against the postmodern promotion of "fragmentation" at the same time that each individual has been parceled into a dozen niches to further the purposes of modern marketing and has been reduced to an instantiation of the general human condition in order to confirm modernity's universal laws of human nature.

Where modernity espouses the imperative always to subsume the particular under an overarching generality, postmodernities resist this gesture in the name of particularity and uniqueness. (Lyotard: "Let us wage a war on totality; let us be witnesses to the unpresentable; let us activate the differences and save the honor of the name."[15]) Postmodern theorists apply their theoretical pressure to the topic of identity at the points where identity falls short, where the fissures open up between (on one hand) the modern scholar's confident claims that two phenomena are the same and (on the other hand) the demonstrable differences between those phenomena.[16] After all, if one can always find difference but must seek out identity by enforcing a limited sphere of attributes that count toward similarity, if we attain identity only by bracketing off acknowledged differences, of what value is the assumption that identity (once again, in the limited sense of sameness) constitutes the primary, undoubtable starting point of reason? What's the value of a limited universal? The modern apologists will insist that scholars should pursue the ideal knowledge of universality, even if we approach this ideal only by way of limited samples. As the following paragraphs illustrate, the postmodern advocates of particularity can present a variety of arguments to the effect that even the most ingenious modern effort to attain the ethereal realm of universality remains in the *diesseitig* (this-sided) world of specifics and differences.

The relation of unique instances to difference and repetition provides one of the motifs for Jacques Derrida's "Signature Event Context."[17] In a portion of the essay that considers the relation of speech-act theory to writing as distinct from speaking, Derrida cites two specific characteristics of linguistic signifiers: they must be able to function in the absence of their author, and they must be repeatable. A writing that could be understood only when its author was present to explain it would not be language as we know it. Only if signifiers serve a communicative end apart from an author's presence to interpret can we recognize them as signifiers. Similarly, an utterly unique signifier—one that could not be repeated, reused, recycled, recirculated—could not function as a signifier at all. How would one learn what it meant? Thus, in order to participate in the network of signification, a signifier must be repeatable. From the structural necessity of absence, Derrida teases out the pervasive effect of *différance*: that is, of the inevitable deferral of meaning and of the similarly inescapable persistence of difference among meanings ascribed to the signifier. From the necessity of repetition, he observes the undecidable oscillation between "same" and "different" in the signifier.

In other words, to produce the signifer Q in this chapter, I consulted the handwritten Q on my manuscript page and depressed the key marked Q on my computer keyboard, at which the computer produced the image of a *Q* on my screen; the computer stored the binary code for *Q*; the computer sent the signal for that binary code to the printer, which in turn reproduced a *Q* on a sheet of paper, which the editors at Fortress Press have transcribed and sent to the printer, where once again the binary code was sent, and the printer formed the requisite *Q*; this *Q*, in turn, was impressed on a photo-offset plate, by which the signifier *Q* was printed onto thousands of sheets of paper. All of these *Q*s are the same; each indisputably is the letter *Q*. Yet all of them are simultaneously different, too. The *Q* on my keyboard is not the *Q* on the screen or on the page, and the *Q* on the manuscript isn't the *Q* on the plate or the *Q* on the printed page, and all the *Q*s on printed pages differ from one another, too. The same? Yes; otherwise we could not recognize them as *Q*s. But all are different as well. My handwritten *Q*, the *Q* key on my computer, the image of a *Q* on the screen, the manuscript *Q*, the offset-plate *Q*, and the final printed *Q* differ from one another in a variety of ways.

Repetition and Difference

Further—and quite apposite to a point that I will develop later—iterability applies not only to isolated signifiers such as letters, but also to words and expressions. Derrida considers this point in order to complicate the account of speech-acts that fuels the theory of communication associated with Austin and Searle, whose speech-act theory systematically excludes "deviant" uses of language such as confessions produced under duress, expressions in a game or on stage, and especially quotation. Where speech-act theory excludes consideration of this form of repetition, of iteration, in order to establish a general theory of speech-acts, Derrida points out that this fundamental exclusion begs the question of whether one can establish rigorous grounds for such a distinction in the first place. On Derrida's account, the quotation itself—the iterated words—differs *as language* only in the ways that every iteration of language always differs from itself. The factors of difference toward which one might point to separate authentic confession from forced confession, or an actual marriage from an operatic marriage, are extrinsic to the linguistic formulations themselves.

Repetition and imitation also find their way into the work of Luce Irigaray, still relatively unfamiliar among theological and biblical scholars.[18] Her philosophical interest lies in unraveling the pernicious social and philosophical effects of male dominance. But rather than focusing her efforts on arguments aimed at establishing "equality" between men and women in the effort to make the differences among people socially invisible, Irigaray argues that the strongest response involves *accentuating* human differences, permitting people to be what they actually are. Irigaray points out that women have been relegated to the margins of philosophy and a broader culture that she characterizes as *monosexual* (wherein women can appear only as "different" or "lesser" men). Women are not truly the Other in these discourses. When the discourses seem to recognize women as Other, they are in fact constructing women as an "Other of the Same," an Other always modeled on and determined by its relation to the Same. (To adopt Irigaray's trope, women gain admission to discourse as reflections in the mirror—the *speculum*—constructed by monosexual discourse.) That being the case, when women try to attain "equality" in status or access, they tacitly acquiesce to the terms of an equality predefined by male domination. Women are, in fact, different from men—physically, psychically, socially—and Irigaray warns her readers that any effort to establish a unity by way of equality will in the end enforce homogeneity of the masculine. Thus, for Irigaray, the question of whether women are "essentially" or "accidentally" different from men is inconsequential; so long as women are different, the characteristics of their difference are *in effect* essential. Irigaray's difference from mainstream feminism lies in her insistence that the path to a better world lies through discovering these differences and activating them, in the interest of evoking a differentiated but harmonic cultural space.

She engages the topic of identity and difference also by a particular practice of philosophical writing, in which she deliberately adopts the voice of "the feminine" (as defined by the theoreticians of monosexual discourse) and endeavors, from that hystericized, irrational, incoherent position to write an undoing of that male-dominated economy of identity. She declines to arm-wrestle the philosophical heavyweights for the prerogative of equality (to men); that would leave the framework of the philosophical systems intact, though with their content amended. Nor will she abstain from participating in the cultural conflicts that bear on women, since that would leave intact the monosexual erasure of women. Instead, she accedes to the space that their discourses allot her, in order to reveal the overdetermined masculinity of their ostensibly neutral philosophies. Irigaray names this tactic mimesis, that is, imitation. She proposes that this sort of imitation provides a basis for women (and any who have been permitted only the status of the Other of the Same) to claim an uncontested cultural staging ground from which to resist the ideological currents that constrain them.

This aspect of Irigaray's interpretive practice resonates with certain pivotal points in Michel de Certeau's essays on interpretation and theology.[19] In both spheres, Certeau weaves an account of difference and repetition especially propitious for theological interpreters of Scripture. Certeau affirms both the value of the particular event and the value of subsequent imitative instantiations of that event. As he observes with regard to the Christian tradition, "However it is taken, Christianity implies a *relationship to the event* which inaugurated it: Jesus Christ. It has had a series of intellectual and social forms which have had two apparently contradictory characteristics: the will to be *faithful* to the inaugural event: the necessity of being *different* from these beginnings."[20] The continuing effort to negotiate this double imperative of repetition and difference constitutes both the problem and the opportunity of Christian faith.

In adherence to the first imperative, the "will to be *faithful*," Christians focus our attention on Jesus Christ, the unique and unsubstitutable occasion of all that follows. We read the scriptural admonitions to "do this in remembrance of me" and to "be imitators of me, as I am of Christ." We speak a language that derives its significance from its reference to the life and effects of Jesus, and always endeavor to sustain a demonstrable continuity with that life and those effects.

In response to the second imperative, the "necessity of being *different*," Christians acknowledge that it is to our advantage that he (Jesus) go away. It is in the absence of Jesus that we receive the Holy Spirit, recognize our consanguinity with sisters and brothers whom we once had thought enemies, and—especially—encounter Jesus anew. Yet we do not encounter Jesus in the same way that Philip and Nathaniel did; difference inhabits our every engagement with Jesus.[21] In a comparable way, our reading of scriptural texts will not put us in the place of the wilderness generation or the apostles, the prophets or the evangelists, or any of their audiences. Instead, we do something *different* with the texts that the biblical authors have left us. (One of the most different things we do is to try, by our application of modern technical interpretive methods, to ascertain exactly what the authors and their audiences made of these texts.[22]) Jesus does not remain present to the church as an idol—"Do not hold on to me," as he commands Mary in John 20:17—but by departing, he makes possible the things greater even than he has done.

This double neg(oti)ation of fidelity and difference issues in an interlocutory practice (something "said-*between*"), making Jesus manifest in "a multiplicity of practices that neither 'preserve' nor repeat the event."[23] We sustain the chain of events inaugurated with the incarnation through the necessarily nonidentical repetition of practices that we identify with Jesus and our forebears.[24] As John Milbank acutely observes, "[Christianity] makes its affirmations about the real, and about 'meaning,' through the constant repetition of a historically emergent practice which has no real point of origination, but only acquires identity and relative stability *through* this repetition."[25] In this sense, our practice of repetition itself *constitutes* the "identity" of that which we are endeavoring to repeat.[26]

To sum up, repetition is not and cannot ever be simply a repetition of the same; repetition always involves difference. The Nicene Creed is not just *the same* when I repeat it in the pew as when a council proposed it (and which council? in what language?), or when Aquinas repeated it, or when our sisters and brothers in Uganda, Japan, or Peru repeat it.[27] While some will object that those differences don't count, these critics will be as unsuccessful as were the advocates of speech-act theory at formulating a general rule that determines how one can tell whether a particular "difference" counts. The ways we decide which differences count are themselves intrinsic to the practice of repetition that Jesus (and Paul) inaugurated, and are, as practiced under contingent circumstances, persistently in flux. We cannot escape difference by a more exacting repetition of a formulation stipulated to be "the same"—though we can and ought to endeavor to give a rich account of why we commend our particular version of repetition.

An Ethic of Repetition

If change rules the temporal world even in our creeds, one might hastily conclude we have no hope of distinguishing faith from folly, hawk from handsaw. Such a conclusion misses the point that humans have continually decided which differences count and which do not, even without successful recourse to a law of identity. The decisions we make may themselves be overturned by time—we might say they are always subject to *reformation*—but that does not make them nondecisions. Many of the church's temporal decisions have been affirmed by the vast preponderance of Christian believers. The residue of theological judgments on which intelligent dissent has rendered consensus unattainable is a testimony to the ambivalence of the church rather than to the meaninglessness of the judgment (or the absence of anything we can call truth). At all times and in all places, Christians distinguish what fits into the faith from what doesn't fit, at the same time aware that all human institutions, even councils and churches, are subject to error. "As the Church of *Jerusalem*, *Alexandria*, and *Antioch* have erred; so also the Church of *Rome* [and we might add, "of *Canterbury*, of *Wittenberg*, of *Geneva*, of *Dallas*"] hath erred, not only in their living and manner of Ceremonies, but also in matters of Faith."[28] Every repetition diverges from its precedents to some extent. Sometimes we decide that such deviation renders the repetition misguided or makes it a new or different thing, and at other times we discern that the difference—indeed, even a succession of accumulated differences—doesn't make a difference. As Stephen Fowl notes, this discernment requires a form of *phronesis* (practical wisdom)—"the activity of noting similarities *and differences* between an exemplar and the particular context in which one tries to live in a manner appropriate to that exemplar."[29] We distinguish orthodox novelty from unacceptable heresy by assessing the gesture in question against the background of elements of a tradition involving beliefs and practices that we share with one another. A point of doctrine is not intrinsically heretical or orthodox, but Christians deem it acceptable or unacceptable depending on where it fits (or doesn't fit) into patterns whose legitimacy is *not* in question at that moment.

These reflections on identity, difference, and repetition enrich the consideration of an ethic of repetition by reminding us that repetition or imitation is not a single thing, a univocal phenomenon that one may simply approve or reject. The characters of *In His Steps* may be faulted for sponsoring an attenuated, optional ethic of the imitation of

Christ—Jesus Lite. Prominent interpretations of Pauline theology have run afoul of Castelli's strictures against the homogenizing impetus to which Paul's admonitions to "be imitators of me" may give rise. A general ethic of the imitation of Christ risks confusing the unique office of Jesus in the economy of salvation with a disciple's more general charge. A trinket marked "WWJD" may trigger an undecided youth to reconsider his evening's plans for debauchery in favor of behavior more fitting for a believer, but it may be more likely to trivialize the crucified Messiah's path of self-renunciation and steadfastness in favor of trendy commercialized spirituality.

Imitation: A Postmodern Prescription

All of these modes of imitation can give rise to suspicion that they sponsor a specious simulacrum of following Jesus, or that they equate faith with a pernicious conformism. They may produce clones or dilettantes in the name of discipleship. Such risks are real; one need only cast a quick glance at the church and its history to recognize Christians' persistent impetus to impose narrow criteria for *legitimate* faith and practice.

Nevertheless, postmodern theorists illustrate a broad range of understandings of imitation, a much broader range than one might infer from the dubious sorts of imitation for which Sheldon may stand as a figurehead. A postmodern reading of scriptural admonitions to follow, to imitate, to repeat provides a basis for fending off the misguided sorts of imitation that either confuse the particularity of our own identities and vocations with the particularity of Jesus (and Paul) or reduce repetition to an occasional, historically haunted rumination over what Jesus would do. Moreover, though our interpretations need not always be determined by historical probabilities, we may opt in this instance to weigh the likelihood of Jesus and Paul imagining that they were implementing a regimen of conformity. Jesus evidently associated with a motley circle; drunks, extortionists, women (notorious and righteous), lunatics, and pagans figure prominently in the stories of who Jesus was and with whom he passed his time. Paul urges his readers to be imitators of him, but on at least one count, he specifically insists that they *not* imitate him. Though he was circumcised on the eighth day, he urges that his male Galatian congregants specifically avoid circumcision. The risk of imposed conformity can be attenuated not only by eschewing Pauline and dominical mimesis, but also by giving imaginative attention to such alternative modes of imitation as the *constitutive repetition* that I commend here.

A positive postmodern practice of repetition may take up the calling to be imitators with an acute awareness that this imitation will not and should not even try to attain identity with its inaugurating precedents. The church bears witness to its mission in changing (geographical and temporal) locales by negotiating its accountability to both identity and difference in ways that can never be fully determined in advance, nor ever escape determination by the examples and instruction of the communion of saints. In response to Jesus' "Do this," contemporary disciples share bread and wine that are certainly not identical to Christ's body and blood, but in which he is nonetheless present. In response to Paul's exhortation to "be imitators of me, as I am of Christ," Paul's sisters and brothers endeavor in ever-different ways to manifest in their lives the gospel of reconciliation, of variegated felicity, of superabundant divine favor that Paul taught. In our differential repetitions, Christians take up Jesus' promise that we would do different—greater—things than what he did, and enact the meaning of his gospel under ever-varying conditions. Such a (postmodern) claim belies the claim that postmodernism evacuates the possibility of ethics. Indeed, it raises the ethical stakes by foregrounding the necessity that interpretation comprise not only academic discourse, but also the lived integrity that backs up hermeneutical claims.[30]

Postmodern discourses offer resources for recognizing coercive dimensions of imitation and repetition (especially in Pauline ethics) to an extent that some thoughtful readers will decline to participate in a movement that seems to require such strict adherence. A different way in postmodern theory, however, reveals fissures in modern discourses of "identity," fissures that belie the assumption that sameness is simply given and that thought merely recognizes an obvious or natural sameness. These fissures are the cracks into which the postmodern wedge enters; the particularity of venturesome believers disrupts the evenness, regularity, and predictability of identity. To the extent that the readership of this essay enters into those disruptions, to the extent that readers are, so to speak, "cracked"—an appropriate condition for such earthen vessels as we—then to this extent, the logic of postmodernism is fulfilled in our ministries, and we have been made fissures of people, called to repeat, differently, the apostolic mission of tuning our ears to the concord by which all the different voices of our sisters and brothers intertwine in a vibrant, shimmering harmony.

CHAPTER SEVEN

The Sign of Jonah: A Fish-Eye View

In recent years, Frank Kermode and Stanley Fish have called our attention to the necessity of considering a proposed interpretation not in isolation, but always with reference to the contexts in which the interpretation was produced and to which it was addressed.[1] The second scholar's name suggests an analogy from the art of photography: A fish-eye view in photography includes in the frame everything in front of the camera. Though the image appears to the viewer to be distorted, there is no optical distortion at all; the curved lines and exaggerated foreground are the mathematically correct representation of what the camera sees. In literary theory, a (Stanley) Fish-eye view includes not only the proposed interpretation in the foreground, but also the background of assumptions that lies behind the proposal. Some would argue that this view introduces a distortion of the interpretive task, but in fact it may eliminate the distortion that can enter the process of interpretation when its presuppositions are unexamined. After outlining this theory of interpretation, I will test the value of a Fish-eye view of Scripture by taking a fish-eye view of the "sign of Jonah" logion.

The Fish-Eye View of Literature

Reminders about the importance of context ought hardly be necessary. When we read so-called precritical exegesis, we must be acutely aware of how the passing of time has affected our understanding of correct interpretation. We behave as if the history of criticism were the history of error, even if we do not believe it. Equally striking differences appear when we compare essays in the *Journal of Biblical Literature* with essays in *Signs* or *The Watchtower*. Our customary explanation of these differences is that *we* know the proper way to interpret, whereas the authors of the past were quaintly credulous or just uninformed, and those who write in journals that differ from ours are tendentious. We assume that precritical exegetes naïvely believed they were discussing actual historical events rather than mythological texts; feminist critics are accused of torturing helpless texts by reading them in the light of "women's experience" rather than the author's intention or the social situation of the community that produced the text. By absolutizing our own standards this way, we create the illusion that they somehow transcend the limitations of our own personal perspectives, an illusion we complete by labeling our exegesis "scientific" or "objective."

Such claims to objectivity are nothing less than a mask for community and personal interests, a whitewash for one particular group's ideology. This tendency may be seen in Michael LaFargue's recent work advocating "value-free" interpretation.[2] While I sympathize with his goals, I cannot agree that these goals are value-free or objective; it is precisely my values that induce me to read in the way they suggest. At the heart of a Fish-eye view of interpretation, then, is the proposal that no objectivity exists in either the method or the object of interpretation, so we necessarily judge interpretations on the basis of our own interests and commitments.

This proposal offends the interpretive profession by suggesting there is no check against willful readers. If their interests and commitments permit them to read *Hamlet* as an allegory of Javanese astrology, then they may do so. Yet what check might there be? Most experts would respond that the text itself is the objective point of reference in question. Anyone who can read can tell that *Hamlet* has no relation whatever to astrology, Javanese or otherwise. However, an appeal to the text so conceived is bound to fail. "The text" has thus far not prevented radical readers from propounding uncanny interpretations. In fact, one generation's outlandish interpretation is often the next generation's stifling orthodoxy, and the third generation's comically dated reading. Kermode cites the example of an introduction to *The Tempest* he wrote in 1954; at the time, it was adjudged fit for the madhouse, while in 1974 it was cited as a concise example of the critical orthodoxy a younger critic sought to overthrow.[3]

This empirical argument for the indeterminacy of interpretation may be balanced by the empirical claim that a text will resist some interpretations while encouraging others. This claim is made (in opposition to Fish's theory) by Gustavo Perez-Firmat, Walter Davis, and Gerald Graff.[4] But we must recognize that the phenomenon of apparent "resistance to interpretation" is not a property inherent in the text but is rather a property of our common propensity to use the English language in certain ways rather than others. Robert Scholes makes a similar point in a discussion of Fish, as does Fish himself in a response to Davis's essay.[5] After all, nothing exists to prevent some determined interpreter from cooking up a way to read adverbs as verbs, verbs as nouns, and so on.[6] The "resistance" argument is not a refutation of Fish-eye readings, but rather a lovely illustration of the way we suppress awareness of our assumptions about interpretation.

The need to emphasize the muteness of the text has led Fish perhaps to overstate his case. He will claim that there is no text, if by text we mean a constant, stable entity to which differing interpretations both appeal. According to Fish, the only text that can be said to exist is "the structure of meanings that is obvious and inescapable from the perspective of whatever interpretive assumptions happen to be in force."[7] I would suggest, however, that a more useful approach would be to concede the (possible) objective existence of the text while denying it any *functional* efficacy. This may please neither Fish, who has fought for nonexistence many times, nor his critics, who want to be able to use the text as a warrant for their arguments. Still, I believe this distinction clarifies what is at issue. Those who accept my formulation will stand with Fish by suggesting that there is no text to demand this interpretation or forbid that one. Those who stand with Fish's critics may be mollified that I do not with a phrase abolish the contents of their bookshelves. Thus, the second point of Fish-eye reading is that while the text as an objective entity presumably exists apart from interpretation, it cannot function as a restraint upon interpretation.

If there is no objective text to interpret, there is likewise no objective method of interpreting. The claims of historical criticism in this regard are grossly misleading. They presuppose first that an interest in history is an objective interest (or a necessary interest—and so, as it were, a "disinterest"). We must see, however, that there is nothing objective whatsoever about such an interest; an interest in history is no more objective than an interest in women's experience. What is more, the "history" to which these critics generally appeal is a projection of their own methodological presuppositions. A historical-critical argument will no longer seem convincing once the methods that produced the picture of history to which that argument appeals have changed. It is helpful in this light to remember that the bulk of Protestant biblical scholarship since the Reformation has made a claim to historical foundation, from the exegesis of the inerrantists to that of the higher critics. In fact, the situation of "history" is just the same as that of the "text": the terms point to some objective thing, but it is inaccessible for the purposes of our arguments. We can only appeal to history or text when all parties to a debate agree on what those might be.

The claim of the historical-critical method to critical rigor is just as shaky. Most members of the historical-critical establishment are critical only insofar as it suits them. They will question the authenticity of Colossians or the historicality of the resurrection, but their critical disposition does not extend to a methodological interrogation of their own presuppositions. They rely on dubious assumptions about the nature of language, literature, knowledge, and ideology. No more do they truly pursue a methodical discipline. They operate by intuition and hunches, with a tacit knowledge of what may or may not be said, but there is no more method in exegesis than in fishing. Whatever beginners may learn as a step-by-step enterprise, they forget upon grasping the underlying patterns of exegetical research.

Instead of treating interpretation as an exercise in objective research, we must see it as a rhetorical exercise directed from within a community of readers to a community of readers. Some interpretations will appear particularly compelling; such readings will rely upon the interpretive conventions that the audience holds in common with the author, and will draw from those conventions the interpretive conclusions that use rules of inference recognized by that audience. There are different rules of inference for feminist interpretation than for historical interpretation (though a feminist historical interpretation may try to hold the two audiences together). Inference from commonly held conventions does not constitute objective criticism; it is simply the strongest possible rhetorical gesture within a field of discourse that values logical inference. A community of Jehovah's Witnesses will accept rhetorical moves that Society of Biblical Literature members would reject. All of this shows, then, that lacking an outside source of authorization for interpretations, readers derive the interpretive authority of their claims from beliefs held in common with other readers, the necessary corollary being that this interpretive authority exists only to the extent that the commonly held beliefs sustain it.

The functional restraints on interpretation begin just where the theoretical restraints are seen to be illusory. The most visible of these restraints include the institutions of accreditation, employment, and publication; less obvious are such forces as the opinions of one's peers. These generally do not restrict interpretation actively. Rather, they screen interpreters, so that "irresponsible" interpreters are not heard in the first place, and they teach interpreters to recognize the sorts of interpretation that are acceptable. Since these institutions are not monolithic or organized, each interpreter will have a slightly different sense of what is acceptable. Some interpreters will think literary theory is utterly irrelevant to biblical criticism; others will concentrate on literary theory, regarding historical work as a tedious subsidiary discipline. These differing critics will ask questions that reflect their particular interests, will admit as evidence materials that suit their definition of relevance, and will consequently arrive at divergent interpretations. Since the contrasting interpretations reflect the interests and presuppositions of their sponsors, it would be a mistake to criticize an interpretation on the basis of commitments that differ from the interpreter's (though one might well, on the basis of shared commitments, call into question a presupposition not held in common). Fish-eye readers will therefore recognize that a reading that proceeds from certain interpretive assumptions cannot admit as justified criticism that proceeds on the basis of different assumptions.[8]

To summarize, then, interpretation is a necessarily subjective, value-laden activity. The text, while possibly existing as an objective set of data, cannot function in interpretation to authorize or rule out given readings apart from the set of interests and presuppositions that interpreters bring to their endeavors. The work of interpretation is not so much methodical as conventional. It is more accurately described as a set of guild rules prohibiting certain interpretive moves and encouraging others. Thus, we must be willing to let go of the ideal of a single correct interpretation toward which the critical endeavor is moving in each text's case. Rather, to evaluate a particular reading productively, we must take into account the interests and presuppositions that guided the interpreter.[9]

Viewing the Sign of Jonah

With these claims in mind, let us undertake a Fish-eye view of the "sign of Jonah" logion. I will treat the logion as a saying of Jesus, not because I am convinced of the historical arguments for its authenticity, but because the very question of its authenticity could not be raised without committing oneself to a set of assumptions from which I would like to distance myself, at least for the purposes of this essay.

While the advantage of a *fish*-eye view is its comprehensive quality, a disadvantage is that details are lost when so much information is crammed into a single frame of film. Images in the foreground appear unduly prominent, while items in the background disappear. In this case, the foreground will emphasize the earliest and most recent readers. I apologize ahead of time for this fault inherent in fish-eye photography, but I expect that anyone who fills in the details I omit will find that they complement the main lines of the picture I present here.

The "sign of Jonah" logion occurs twice in Matthew and once in Luke. In the simplest case, Pharisees and Sadducees request a sign from Jesus, to which request he answers, "An evil and adulterous generation asks for a sign, but no sign will be given to it except the sign of Jonah" (Matt. 16:4). (We need not concern ourselves here with the textual status of the "signs of the times" logion.) Each of the other two occurrences offers some explanation of the sign. Earlier in Matthew, some scribes and Pharisees ask for the sign, and Jesus adds to the response, "For just as Jonah was three days and three nights in the belly of the sea monster, so for three days and three nights the Son of Man will be in the heart of the earth" (Matt. 12:40). In the final case, in Luke, Jesus speaks "when the crowds were increasing," and this time he explains the sign by saying, "For just as Jonah became a sign to the people of Nineveh, so the Son of Man will be to this generation" (Luke 11:29–30).

Thus, we are presented with two main options: either Jesus claimed that the sign of Jonah involved the prophet's three-day sojourn in the whale's belly, which in some way prefigures a comparable descent by the Son of Man, or he associated the sign of Jonah with the prophet's relation to the people of Nineveh, which prefigures the Son of Man's relation to his own generation. In neither case is the exact nature of the sign clear, so interpreters have from the beginning sought to clarify the meaning of Jesus' obscure reference.

The very earliest attempts focused on Matthew's version of the saying, probably because it provided a self-verification of Jesus' resurrection. Justin Martyr and Cyprian both cite this example in their controversies with Jewish opponents.[10] Here Jesus offered a prophecy that his own fate would mirror the fate of an Old Testament prophet, lending the cachet of ancient testimony to his mission, and later events bore out his prediction, thus confirming his credentials as a man of supernatural insight. But Matthew's version of the saying also presented a serious problem, inasmuch as Jesus did *not* spend three days and three nights in the heart of the earth. This is the crux of the earliest interpretations of the sign of Jonah. The *Gospel of the Nazarenes*, for example, is supposed to have omitted the embarrassing "three days" clause.[11] The Syriac *Didascalia Apostolorum* argued that actually Jesus was in the tomb three days and three nights; the morning of Good Friday counted as one day, the darkness at noon as one night, the afternoon as another day, the night as the second night, and then the Sabbath day and night made three.[12] Later critics would often substitute the familiar "on the third day" for the awkward "three days and three nights."[13] Or they identified the "three days and three nights" reference as synecdoche (the parts of Friday, Saturday, and Sunday count for the whole of three days and nights). The earliest such reference I have found is in Tyconius's *Book of Rules*, followed by the letter of Alcuin to Charlemagne in the year 798.[14] R. H. Gundry suggests that this was a customary way of describing the passage of time.[15] Or the phrase was an estimate—after all, Jonah couldn't have known how much time had passed. (Martin Luther notices this in his *Lectures on Jonah.*[16]) Finally, it is possible to suggest that "three days and three nights" was to Matthew's audience no more specific than "a day or two" is to us. (However, Gundry considers this argument dubious.[17])

The association of the sign of Jonah with the resurrection became firm and popular. Thus, Jonah is frequently associated with Shadrach, Meshach, and Abednego as symbols of resurrection. Likewise, Jonah's being delivered from the whale is a favorite scene in early iconography. In an anonymous poem on Jonah, the prophet is described as

> a sign hereafter of the Lord—
> A witness was he
> Not of destruction, but of death's repulse.[18]

The growth of iconographic and poetic traditions interpreting the sign of Jonah was paralleled by increasing breadth of interpretation. So Irenaeus did not simply reiterate the saying or explicate the chronology of the resurrection, but expanded and shifted the interpretation of the sign. In *Against Heresies*, the whale is the devil, "author of all transgressions," and Jonah represents the human. The whale can swallow up but not utterly destroy the human. The sign of Jonah is the sign of submission to the Lord God, by which submission we, too, may rise from the dead.[19]

This would make a natural transition to the allegorical interpretation with which Origen is identified. Oddly enough, however, Origen shows little interest in the sign; he does not even mention it in his extended comparison of Jonah and Jesus (I have found no other reference to Jonah in Origen than *Contra Celsus* 7.57—not 8.57, as Bowers suggests on p. 24). It was Origen's great opponent Methodius of Olympus who found an allegorical meaning of the sign. He explains that the whale signifies time, which consumes all things, and that Jonah signifies Adam, since both men fell from life into death. The three days and three nights signify "the three stages of our present life on earth, that is, the beginning, the middle and the end, of which all this present time consists." The sign of Jonah is Christ's descent to the world and death, that he might bring us to eternal life. If we meditate on the figurative meaning of the prophet's career, wrote Methodius, we will see that it all boils down to this.[20] Jerome extended typological connections to Jonah's name: "According to tropology, Jonah signifies Our Lord, that is to say 'a dove,' or the 'sad one' . . . since the Holy Ghost descends in the form of a dove, or since he sorrows for our sins, and weeps for Jerusalem so that we might be cleansed of maculation."[21] Moreover, Jonah's shipwreck "prefigures the Passion of Our Lord who calls the entire world to penitence: and in the name of Nineveh Jonah as a type of Christ proclaims salvation to all the Gentiles."[22] Bede adds, "Nineveh should be interpreted as the splendid; it signifies the Church ornate with the glory of all virtue."[23] Haymo of Halberstadt expands this by identifying Nineveh with "the congregation of all people, the carnal and the spiritual, as well as an infinite number of beasts which signify the irrational creatures who serve their belly, regard the world, practice cupidity, and never look up to Heaven."[24]

Before proceeding to the twentieth century, I call attention to the presuppositions and interest of the early interpreters we have surveyed. First, none of these interpreters raises any questions about the historicity either of Jonah's adventure or of the possibility of Jesus' predicting his own resurrection (let alone the genuineness of the logion). Second, there is little hesitation, at least among the earliest interpreters, to ascribe nonliteral signification to the pericope. Whereas a naïve reader might mistakenly think Jesus was simply talking about a prophet and a cetacean, an acute interpreter like Haymo could ascertain an elaborate system of reference. Third, the emphasis in these interpretations is heavily on Matthew's interpretation of the sign.

Still, the problem won't go away. While Luke's interpretation is less clearly supernatural, it is likewise less clear. So to this day, curiosity about the sign of Jonah is unabated, and the proposals about its meaning comprise a variety such as we have not seen since the early Middle Ages. At the turn of the century, B. W. Bacon proposed that the sign of Jonah was really the sign of John the Baptist, Jonah being either a corruption of Johanon or a pun, and that by the sign Jesus refers to their mutual preaching of repentance.[25] According to Bultmann, the sign of Jonah is that as Jonah came to Nineveh from a distant country, so the Son of Man will descend from heaven.[26] Jeremias's article' "Ἰωνᾶς" in the *Theological Dictionary of the New Testament* suggests that the sign "consist[s] in the authorization of the divine messenger by deliverance from death,"[27] on the assumption that the Ninevites somehow knew that Jonah had been so delivered. In the context of Jesus' preaching, then, the sign is "a riddle. The sign of Jonah will be renewed with the manifestation of the Son of Man returning from the dead."[28] But Dom John Howton argues that the sign of Jonah is "the sign of the dove," in this case not Jonah's name but the dove as a symbol of the Spirit, among other things.[29] Perhaps Eugene Merrill is right, and the sign of Jonah is the sign of a man delivered from a great fish to a city (Nineveh) founded by a fish-god (Nanshe).[30] We may accept Landes's argument that in Matthew the saying means, "As Jonah was, so will the Son of Man be in the netherworld acclaiming the divine liberation from death,"[31] but that in Luke it should be interpreted as "[Jonah's] proclamation of judgment, for it was to that that all the Ninevites responded."[32] Or we may with Pierre Bonnard define the sign of Jonah as "the judgment of God."[33]

Of course, these suggestions are more complex than I could possibly convey within the limits of this discussion. But after all, the point of this essay is not to justify these claims, but rather to show the variety of claims that have been presented. I assure you that none is frivolous. All are carefully argued, and their frequent citations of the scholarly literature indicate that they are addressed to a discerning audience.

Nonetheless, the variety they reflect is real. Scholarly erudition has not led to critical convergence. This takes us back to our starting place: what does the sign of Jonah mean?

Implications of the Fish-Eye View

If you have retained in mind my claims from the first part of this chapter, you will see how this Fish-eye view of the history of the sign of Jonah confirms those proposals. While some might argue that with historical-critical methods we have finally entered an age of objective interpretation, I am hard-pressed to find a basis for that claim. It is least easily justified by what would be the natural fruits of such objectivity, that is, some consensus on the meaning of the sign. The presumably objective text has not discernibly restrained interpretation. The interpreters I've discussed have not followed a methodical process that led to assured results; their operations have been governed by their own sense of what the text *might* mean, a sense they held in common with contemporary readers.

One of the most powerful presuppositions that directed interpretation of the sign has been the interpreter's understanding of history. Among the patristic interpreters, we can see little doubt that Jonah was cast off a boat and swallowed by a great fish, surviving miraculously for about seventy-two hours, and that Jesus might have been able to predict that he would experience a similar entombment. Among the modern interpreters, only one (Merrill) puts any stock in the historicity of Jonah's story, and the possibility of Jesus foretelling his fate is treated rationalistically where it is considered at all. This change makes all the difference in the world. If Jonah was fictional and Jesus was not prescient, readers simply cannot seriously propose the interpretations that seemed obvious in the first century. If, in contrast, we admit only that Jesus *might* have predicted that he would rise three days after having been killed (a point that the Gospels stress), there is no great obstacle to believing that he compared himself to Jonah with regard to those three days, and whether Jonah was a historical personage is irrelevant. Neither view of what might be historical can point to a basis other than "what we can believe." Nowadays most people can't believe that Jonah survived in a fish or that Jesus predicted his resurrection, but we can't point to some "fact" that supports this disbelief. At this end of the interpretive record, we cannot see a gradual progress toward the single meaning of the sign, but only the waxing and waning of interpretive trends.

The waning of a set of interpretive commitments is not the same as a Kuhnian paradigm shift, as Walter Wink, Elizabeth Schüssler Fiorenza, and others have claimed.[34] In fact, it has much more in common with the fashion industry, in which novelties are constantly introduced and advocated by professional innovators. While the outlandish extremes are not retained, their influence always affects what people wear, sometimes drastically. While avant-garde interpreters may come to meetings dressed as deconstruction workers, historical criticism will remain the gray flannel suit of interpretation, and the rest of us will try to fit in somewhere in between.

By way of a concluding illustration, allow me to suggest a classroom scene. The professor is imparting the nuances of legitimate biblical interpretation. One student, toward the back, asks the professor, "But what is the anagogical meaning of the sign of Jonah?" If our classroom is set in the eighth century, the teacher will explain in detail the way the sign prefigures some eschatological reality. If the same question were asked in a twentieth-century classroom, the teacher would stare out the window, take a deep breath, and wonder how on earth to handle this off-the-wall inquiry.

But why? Is "What is the anagogical meaning of the sign of Jonah?" really a less worthy, less reasonable question than "Isn't this saying most likely a creation of the early church?" Each makes perfect sense to some community. Tropologically, the sign of Jonah may well be the sign of the sad one who sorrows for our sins; historically, it may be the sign of the judgment of God. But neither interpretation is privileged by the nature of the approach. If we are to justify the belief that our approach is better than someone else's, we must somehow weigh the two sets of interests reflected by the approaches. And I am not persuaded that if such an evaluation were possible, there would be seen any compelling reason to opt for historical criticism rather than the fourfold system of the Middle Ages.

If, then, we adopt this Fish-eye view of interpretation, does the ideal of correct interpretation vanish? Yes, it does, but only in the abstract, where it never did us any good anyway. "Correct interpretation" can still be invoked, but only in a limited way, by appeal to mutually recognized norms of interpretation. Those who wish to judge interpretations will have to judge by standards to which those interpretations implicitly or explicitly appeal, or else acknowledge the possible disjunction between the critic's and the interpreter's commitments. The fact is that we will find ourselves agreeing about many more aspects of a text than we disagree about. Just as no reader of this article really expected an ichthyological perspective on the text, so no reader will argue that the sign of Jonah was a placard the prophet carried. If we limit the bases of our arguments to commonly held assumptions, if we use our terms and ideas in a common sense, we will have mutually agreed-upon standards for correct interpretation, and on their basis we will be able to judge some interpretations of the sign of Jonah correct and others incorrect.

It is perhaps paradoxical that an article advocating the widespread adoption of a theoretical position widely perceived to be antitraditional concludes by claiming that just this theory impels willing interpreters to a keener awareness of the traditions in which they stand. Nonetheless, the careful examination of a Fish-eye view of the sign of Jonah as it was interpreted through the centuries served to confirm the claim that community interests direct interpretive practice.

When the assumptions we hold about interpretation are subjected to as much scrutiny as our interpretations themselves, we are reminded of how much in our interpretation we owe to our precursors and our colleagues. In retrospect, we can see that this is what Matthew and Luke showed that Jesus did in referring to the sign of Jonah: he called attention to the tradition in which he stood, which he would reenact and, at the same time, create anew. In prospect, we can see that the sign of Jonah is the sign of our being swallowed up by a big Fish that (after we plead for salvation) regurgitates us, safe on shore, to go about the business to which we have been called.

CHAPTER EIGHT

Disciples Together, Constantly: Reading in Community

Several years ago, the leadership of the Episcopal Church undertook a parish-based study of human sexuality. The House of Bishops sought guidance from all Episcopalians regarding the theological status of nonmarital sexual intimacy. When my own home parish discussed what the church should say about homosexuality and sexual activity outside marriage, participants in the discussion group frequently expressed annoyance with the entire process. "Why does God care about who I sleep with?" Some responded to their own question with the words of the old song, "Ain't nobody's business but my own," even though this presumptuously banishes the God to whom (in the words of the Anglican Collect for Purity) "all hearts are open, all desires are known, and from whom no secrets are hid" from involvement in our sexual lives. Other participants flattened the complexity of theological deliberation into the bald assertion, "If the Bible says it, we have to do it."[1]

Neither party, however, exercised the gift and vocation of theological discernment to justify their arguments. They ignored the initial question ("Why does God care?") and simply claimed either that God was irrelevant to their sexual behavior or that God had established unambiguous guidelines for God's own reasons. Their impulse to ask why God cares was wiser than their conclusions, though. Whatever we have to say about God's will for our sexual lives, we ought to be able to give some account of what God's interest in our intimate relationships might be.

One common answer draws on the Levitical rationale, "You shall be holy, for I the LORD your God am holy" (Lev. 19:2). This has the merit of strong scriptural support, but it unfortunately defers the question more than it answers it. We are still left wondering what makes some forms of sexual behavior holy, others unholy, and what that has to do with God's own holiness. We may, as an alternative, draw on the scriptural natural-law tradition[2] to argue that only "natural" sex is theologically legitimate, though this approach entails problems of its own. Yet a third position submits that lesbian and gay Christians have a right to equal access to sacramental blessing of their relationships.

All three of these responses presuppose that the relevant question is, What are we to say about homosexuality and sexual activity outside marriage? Such a starting point, however, obscures the importance of understanding the ethical status of *all* intimate human relationships. My own approach seeks the basis for our sexual ethics in the character of relationships that God initiates and commends to us: our relationships with all people should conform to God's relationship with Jesus, Israel, and the church. On this account, we are called to make our relationships with one another honest, faithful, self-giving, and constant. This proposal recognizes the theological soundness of some relationships that the churches now condemn and puts hard questions to some relationships that the churches now bless, but it provides a scriptural basis for assessing the various dimensions of human sexuality and offers a way forward that depends neither on a breezy acceptance of secular standards nor on the perpetuation of ecclesiastical ethical habits that could be subject to faithful reformation.

Intimate Relationships: Common Criteria

The first option, which stresses the holiness of certain specified sexual practices, has the benefit of relative clarity. It has likewise been adopted into the law codes of many civil juris-dictions. This position appeals to the injunctions against same-sex intimacy in Leviticus: "You shall not lie with a male as with a woman" (18:22; cf. Lev. 20:13). While there is much to be said concerning this verse, in this context its chief drawback is that it lacks a clear theological rationale. The Levitical dictum identifies itself clearly as God's will but does not amplify the character of that will apart from God's holiness. Some readers will find this an advantage, inasmuch as this distinct statement of God's will may be less subject to interpretive quibbling.

At the same time, however, even the compendious laws of sexual holiness fail to consider some sexual practices (same-sex intimacy among women, for one example). Moreover, the statutes of Levitical holiness also demand a panoply of dietary and social practices that contemporary Christians no longer feel obliged to honor. If, for instance, the Levitical taboo on male homosexual relations is eternally binding, then there is no obvious reason that we should permit the cross-breeding of animals or the blending of fabrics (Lev. 19:19), tattoos (Lev. 19:28), Sabbath breaking (Lev. 19:3; 23:3), or any landholding beyond the limits of the fifty-year jubilee (except, of course, in walled cities; Leviticus 25). The Holiness Code makes no distinction between jubilary economics and normative heterosexuality: both are equally manifestations of God's holiness. The strength of the holi-ness law should be its absoluteness, but it appears that "holi-ness" is still not a sufficient ethical criterion for outlawing homosexual intimacy. Those who would appeal to the law to prohibit homosexual intimacy need supplemental legislation to cover certain sexual acts and likewise need a theoretical justification for adopting some absolutes from the Holiness Code while utterly disregarding others.

The tradition that draws its warrants from what we might call natural law entails its own complications. Does "natural" refer to a scientifically definable principle or to God's intention for creation? If the former, we must admit that nature's message on homosexual intimacy is lamentably equivocal; scientists have attained no clarity in their efforts to discern what "natural sexual relations" might be.[3] Partisans of every position accuse their opponents of permitting ideological considerations to taint the scientific precision of their research. If "natural" identifies God's will for creation in a way that may conflict with the conclusions of the empirical sciences, we need to elaborate what the relation is between God's will and nature, and how we ascertain what God's will might be. In either case, a natural-law approach leaves us without a clear answer to the question of what *aspect* of our sexual behavior warrants God's commendation or condemnation.

The third approach, which treats Christian sexual ethics as a matter of human rights, has tremendous appeal in the cultural climate of liberal democracy. One can appeal to Pauline texts such as Galatians 3:28 and Colossians 3:11, to the effect that distinctions such as male and female, slave and free, Jew and Gentile, and (in this case) gay and straight are irrelevant to those who have been made one in the body of Christ. This approach begs the question, however. This view of sexuality *presupposes* that homosexuality is simply given, as is biological gender or ethnic identity, but those who resist ecclesiastical accommodation to homosexual activity argue that it is a form of behavior contrary to God's will for humanity. The voices for normative heterosexuality may point out that one would not say, "In Christ there is neither murderer nor victim, neither oppressor nor oppressed." Moreover, the entire matter of human rights is complicated for disciples of a Christ who renounced his privileges and came as a slave to serve humanity. Finally, however, this "ecclesiastical rights" argument—like the other perspectives we have scanned—fails to clarify what interest God has in our intimate relationships, so it effectively leaves Christians speechless when they are called upon to give an account of the ethical judgments they make.

Intimate Relationships: Why God Cares

Why *does* God care about our relationships? First, God cares because the character of our relationships with one another is inseparable from the character of our relationship with God. This is one implication of Jesus' teaching in the Gospel of Matthew. There Jesus teaches us that in showing hospitality to others, we show hospitality to him; in clothing the naked, feeding the hungry, visiting the prisoners, we do the same to Jesus (Matthew 25). We cannot be hard-hearted to our neighbors and warmhearted to God; we cannot be fickle to our loved ones and faithful to God. The intensity and intimacy of a relationship increase its importance as a barometer of our relation to God. Thus, God cares about our relationships with one another because God cares about our relationship with God.

The church has conventionally subjected extramarital relationships to ethical scrutiny, while it has regarded marriage itself as a known and approved condition. I suggest, however, that we examine all relationships of human intimacy together. If we limit our deliberation about sexual behavior only to extramarital relationships, we introduce a persistent distortion into our ethical deliberation. On one hand, marital relationships can provide crucial evidence for theologically approved human intimacy; on the other hand, marriage does not guarantee that a given relationship is sound, since marriage can in some cases simply provide a façade of legitimacy for a superficial or even malignant relationship.

When we opt to make marriage—rather than non-marital relationships—the starting point for deliberating about the ethical status of intimate relationships, we have direct testimony attributed to Jesus and Paul. The Synoptic Gospels (Matthew, Mark, and Luke) show Jesus addressing the topic of marriage on two occasions: the first when he discusses divorce and the second when he confronts the Sadducees concerning levirate marriage (the obligation of a widow's brother-in-law to beget a son for her, so that her family would have a male heir). Paul discusses marriage in a tremendous variety of contexts, from the binding force of the law to mixed marriages to apostolic privilege. One striking feature of these various discussions is that the theological weight in each case falls on marriage's character as a commitment that binds two people together for life.

LIFETIME COMMITMENT

Indeed, Jesus and Paul stress both the importance and the limitations of the lifetime commitment. Those who take marriage vows are making a lifelong commitment: "They are no longer two, but one flesh. Therefore what God has joined together, let no one separate" (Matt. 19:6). Likewise, Paul emphasizes that marriage is indissoluble (1 Corinthians 7, repudiating divorce in vv. 10–11; and Rom. 7:2–3). By the same token, marriage is a strictly mundane matter ("Those who belong to this age marry and are given in marriage," Luke 20:34). Widows and widowers are released from their obligation to their spouses, and marital obligations are not pertinent to the eschatological dimension of human existence ("Those who are considered worthy of a place in that age and in the resurrection from the dead neither marry nor are given in marriage. Indeed they cannot die anymore, because they are like angels and are children of God, being children of the resurrection," Luke 20:35–36). Paul seems to imagine that his preference for celibacy is a sort of preparation for this nonconjugal heavenly life. In short, marriage is ordained as a terrestrial institution, binding for life upon those who undertake it, but its jurisdiction does not extend to the heavenly dimension of believers' lives.

Now, Paul and Jesus do not make the point that marriage is lifelong as a casual digression or as a simple illustration. They take the institution of marriage—itself a condition commended by God in creation, but blended in a peculiar amalgam with a secular institution familiar in the political life of most societies—and anchor its theological significance in the rationale of unity and constancy that they knew from the book of Genesis. In the Gospels and Letters, the leaders of the early church thus articulate a crucial theological justification for their approach to marriage. Marriage involves the spouses in the creation of a new relational identity that is given, sustained, and sealed by God. This new relation has a variety of civic and pragmatic dimensions (defining units of population, production, and dependency, the generation and sustenance of offspring, and so on), but its principal theological dimension is constituted by lifelong fidelity: 'For this reason a man shall leave his father and mother and be joined to his wife, and the two shall become one flesh.' . . . Therefore what God has joined together, let no one separate" (Matt. 19:5–6). People whom God joins in marriage cannot, on their own initiative, break the bond of marriage, any more than humans can annul God's covenant with Israel. Indeed, the marital covenant is an icon of the covenant of grace between God and humanity, as illustrated by the force of marriage metaphors in Scripture (Isa. 54:5; 62:1–5; Jeremiah 3; Ezek. 16:8; Hos. 2:19–20; and Mal. 2:11),[4] likewise the metaphors of Christ as spouse of all believers (Matt. 9:15; 25:1–6; John 3:2b–3; 2 Cor. 11:2; Eph. 5:25–27; and Rev. 19:7; 21:2, 9).

In other words, Scripture repeatedly makes the theological point that relations of utmost human intimacy ought to communicate something about God's relation to humanity. The particular point that most permeates biblical uses of the analogy of marriage is that God's love for God's people is manifest in a constant, undying commitment,[5] so our relationships with one another, when we avow them in a theological context, should be constant and undying. If we shortchange the powerful testimony of Jesus and Paul to the importance of constancy in our most intimate relationships, we betray an opportunity to testify by our lives to God's avowed commitment to us.

Commitment and Gender

God's commitment to us is not based on gender distinction. When God espouses Israel, when Jesus is bridegroom to the church, they do not commit themselves only to people of one gender. God's call to discipleship and concomitant promise of salvation are offered to all people. Though in the past (and in some quarters today), full participation in the body of Christ was conditional upon maleness, many churches have recognized that women also have places in ordained ministry and church leadership. So, too, full participation in church life has hitherto been limited to people with (real or feigned) heterosexual inclinations, though the gifts and the calling of God do not depend on the gender of the people to whom the disciple is sexually attracted. On the contrary, God makes a vow of covenanted constancy to *all* who are willing to receive that covenant, as the biblical writers repeatedly illustrate with the metaphor of God's marrying God's people. The significance of marriage as a biblical metaphor lies in the assumption that the marital relation epitomizes the quality of mutual intimacy and fidelity in human relationship. When we see married disciples of Jesus living lives of shared commitment to one another and to the gospel, we encounter one of the most vivid material illustrations of God's faithful love for us.

Applying the Constancy Criterion

On this account, the central theological importance of marriage as the church's institution for the blessing and support of human intimacy lies in *constancy*. Only our trust in God's constancy can make possible the radical commitment that accepts Jesus' call to discipleship (calling us to give over every element of our lives in the service of our sisters and brothers, placing all our trust in God's care for us). Likewise, only our trust in a spouse's constancy can make possible a radical commitment to a relationship whose theological significance lies in its capacity to represent God's self-giving, forgiving, intimate, constant love for us.

What is the relevance of this criterion for judging whether particular relationships are fittingly blessed by the church's approbation? Firstly, and probably most uncomfortably, the criterion of constancy calls into question the ease with which American churches have made their peace with the phenomenon of remarriage after divorce.[6] Christians ought to manifest more appreciation for the tremendous effort that faithful matrimony requires, more sympathy for the humiliation and frustration and spiritual pain that failed marriages incur, and more critical caution regarding the possibility that projected marriages succeed. Even though our cultural climate inclines us to keep our noses out of our neighbors' affairs, our role as witnesses to and supporters of a marriage obliges us to speak frankly if we see impediments to the successful sustenance of the marriage. Many who have wrought long marital relationships testify that the effort requires a great deal from the participants and their friends. To the extent that the church recognizes the importance of emphasizing that marriage entails a genuine commitment to mutual constancy, Christians will need to work together to sustain marriages and sympathetically understand divorce.

Secondly, the criterion of constancy directs the church's attention away from its habitual scrupulous fascination with genital sexuality. Most Christians are willing to welcome, approve, and ordain lesbian and gay members *so long as* they do not engage in genital sexual relationships (that is, so long as they do not "practice" their sexuality, as if sexual identity were of ethical significance only in moments of genital contact—would hand-holding count?). There are countless ways in which human relationships can fall short of God's ideal, and these do not depend on the matter of who does what with whose genitals. Our relationships can be marred by violence committed by one partner against the other. Our relationships can be tainted with a deep current of self-interest that makes of one's partner simply a commodity for gratifying particular carnal and psychological needs, so that if we are no longer delighted by our partners or if we outgrow them, we feel justified in breaking off our relationships with them and seeking out a new, more satisfying package. Our relationships can be warped by our conviction that each of us should protect a private, individual dimension of our lives, for which we are not accountable to those we love. We make commitments with and call for trust from people to whom we are unwilling to entrust our whole selves. All of these tendencies debase relations of human intimacy without regard to who is intimate with whom, and the cultural ascendancy of these tendencies makes true, honest, constant commitments all the more difficult to sustain.

Thirdly, the criterion of constancy provides some answers to the questions raised against each of the other proposed approaches. Relations that do not respect the criterion of constancy violate God's holiness, for they profess to represent God's steadfast love to the world but instead represent our all-too-human incapacity to fulfill the promises we make. The notion that same-sex couples could manifest godly constancy was alien to the people of ancient Israel, as it is to many today. If we do not rule out such relationships from the beginning of our deliberations, however, we may find that such couples have been abiding in our midst unbeknownst to us.

The natural-law argument against homosexual intimacy in Paul has the same status as his natural-law argument against men having long hair. Paul, like the rest of us, repudiates as "unnatural" that which his culture has excluded as taboo.[7] The list of acts that have been deemed unnatural at one time or another, by one or another social group, would prohibit practically every form of human endeavor. Indeed, much behavior that lies at the heart of Christian discipleship is profoundly unnatural. Only a naïvely romantic view would suggest that we are naturally peaceable, gentle, willing to yield, full of mercy and good fruits, without a trace of partiality or hostility; the Letter of James identifies these as the effects of a wisdom that comes to us from heaven (3:17), contrasted with the "earthly, unspiritual, devilish" traits of envy, ambition, disorder, and wickedness.

There is no need for defenders of lesbian and gay Christians to appeal to a notion of ecclesiastical rights if we hold up constancy as a criterion of human relationships. Constancy comes in relationships of all kinds, even in intimate sexual relationships against which there are forceful legal, ecclesiastical, and social sanctions. The fact that some gay and lesbian Christians have sustained committed relationships over many years, despite the active opposition that such relationships provoke in many quarters, testifies to an admirable and rare sense of constant fidelity (a constancy that is all the more striking in the many partners who have undertaken overwhelming responsibilities to nurse their beloved through the devastating effects of AIDS).

What then shall we say? Should the church bless committed relationships that bespeak constancy and love, when those relationships involve couples of the same sex? In the few passages where Scripture addresses the topic directly, it says no. At the same time, the institution of marriage is clearly a human institution, which changes as the Spirit leads us into all truth and as we change our social relations with one another. Whatever else may be true, all participants in the theological discussion of human sexuality should be ready to acknowledge that the institution of marriage has been in constant, gradual change throughout the history of Israel and the church. In Genesis we find polygynous marriages wherein women were valued as objects of exchange. Abraham's servant obtains Rebekah in exchange for jewels, money, and fine garments (Genesis 24), and Jacob exchanges seven years' labor for Leah, then another seven years' labor for Rachel (Genesis 29). The Torah commands that if a husband dies and leaves his wife without a son, his brother-in-law must beget a son for the widow. The household codes in New Testament epistles authorize men to exercise domination over their wives.

Yet few (if any) churches hold up a model of marriage drawn from Abrahamic or Mosaic texts, and most churches repudiate the male-dominant cast of Pauline marital rhetoric. God's people have amended the institution of marriage as they have discerned elements in it that do not harmonize with other dimensions of Christian life. The mutability of marriage is fitting and good for God's people. As Jesus points out, we marry as those who belong to this age, though marriage is irrelevant with respect to the resurrection life (Luke 20:34). The church's definition of marriage contains no inherent reason not to permit change with respect to same-sex couples when we have changed the marital institution in so many other respects.

Christians therefore must discern whether arguments on behalf of blessing same-sex couples' relationships outweigh the reasons adduced to continue prohibiting such blessings. When familiar arguments about holiness, nature, and rights lead us to an impasse, the criterion of constancy may provide a clear, practical, theologically powerful touchstone for distinguishing intimacies that the church can affirm and support from intimacies that the church must resist. We must deliberate, pray, and examine our consciences, lest prejudice or self-interest predetermine our conclusions, and we must seek the mind of Christ to ascertain what best befits God's people. In short, we need to think seriously about precisely the question that my home parish's discussion group short-circuited.

Conclusion

Why does God care about our sexual lives? Perhaps because the ways that we order our sexual lives signal our highest priorities, our deepest sense of who we are and to whom we can be loyal and true. Some Christians would say that a couple who have vowed perpetual fidelity, who dedicate their lives to the well-being of their neighbors, who endure exclusion and hardship but persevere in faith, who forgive those who persecute them and who love their enemies, who participate as fully in the life of the church as they are permitted, and who patiently, lovingly embody the covenant of constancy that God has made with all of us ought not to be granted the church's blessing on the relationship of mutual trust and support that undergirds their discipleship. Some might even say that such a commitment is impossible, merely illusory, and that the façade of constancy conceals a rotten structure of depravity. Others—myself included—can only bear witness to what we have heard, what we have seen with our eyes, what we have beheld and touched with our hands concerning the lives of exemplary discipleship that our sisters and brothers have shared with us. Such lives bring glory to the God of heaven and earth, such lives are everybody's business, and we are all impoverished if we do not extend to these holy sisters and brothers the church's support for their commitment to constant discipleship.

Signifying Theology

He placed himself in the order of signs.
—Maurice de la Taille

No one has ever seen God. It is God the only Son, who is close to the Father's heart, who has made him known.
—John 1:18

A great preponderance of the literature concerning exegesis and theology begins from the premise that these two endeavors differ in such important, constitutive ways that they require a special discourse dedicated to explaining and remedying their divergence. I will refrain from trying to convince my readers that this premise has not always seemed self-evident to the most sophisticated exegetes and theologians (who until recent years frequently turned out to be the same people). Nor will I suggest we can simply pretend that the nineteenth and twentieth centuries never happened, and return ourselves intellectually and spiritually to a fantasy of how an exegete-theologian of bygone years must have thought. Rather, I will point to elements of these separated-sibling discourses that provide the possibility of finding a renewed convergence, and will sketch a way of imagining exegesis and theology in an integrated discourse.

Elsewhere I have argued that theologians and biblical interpreters who care about a clearer connection between exegesis and theology ought to consider their theological reading as a *signifying practice*, a deliberate intervention in the economy of signification, toward the end of articulating an understanding of the gospel in a lived expression.[1] The key concept of "signifying practice" offers the theological interpreter several advantages, including a multifaceted way to envision exegesis and theology as complementary aspects of an integrated pursuit.

Let us consider this advantage in the context of my two epigraphs: the phrase that Maurice de la Taille applied to God's initiative in the incarnation ("He placed himself in the order of signs")[2] and John 1:18 ("No one has ever seen God. It is God the only Son, who is close to the Father's heart, who has made him known"). Students of the Greek text of John will immediately recall that John writes that the incarnate Word *exēgēsato* the Father, "exegeted" God. I hasten to repudiate the temptation to torture the sense of *exēgēsato* to equal the "exegesis" sought by academic papers in biblical studies; our exegesis is more technical and narrow than the activity John ascribes to the Word. If, however, we read the verb in question with greater lexicographic precision—whether as "expound" or "interpret," "narrate" or "describe"[3]—it fits aptly our work of expounding, interpreting, narrating, describing the character of God via the complementary exercise of textual exegesis and reflective theology. Moreover, especially, by imagining God's incarnational intervention in the economy of signification as a model and vehicle for our own exposition of the Truth,[4] we can more soundly coordinate our study of Scripture and our reflection on doctrine to strengthen each other.

This suggestion depends first of all on the presumption that theology and exegesis do indeed somehow hang together. Certainly many contemporary practitioners of theology and exegesis dissent from that presumption, and their grounds have been made clear often enough. At the same time, we have historic reasons for supposing that this need not be the case, and I doubt we will come to understand the convergence of exegesis and theology if we begin from their disjunction. If we can attain such a convergence, it will be by envisioning the complementarity of these two distinct discourses and exploring how we might make that possibility real.

So that the case for convergence may carry conviction, however, we must attend to the causes that have provoked so persistent an investment in the separation of discursive powers. The two academic discourses have developed defensive antipathies against one another on the basis of real experiences of disruptive intervention. Biblical scholars learn from their disciplinary history that theologians are likely to demand that the Bible be forced to yield only those interpretations that meet dogmatic criteria of legitimacy, or to affirm a greater degree of positivity than the conventions of technical interpretive analysis permit. Theologians (and here I'm partly guessing) learn that biblical scholars devote endless attention to minutiae, or that they insist theologians rely on "assured results" whose half-lives compare unfavorably to the durations of popular television series or sports dynasties. The particular complaints each party might bring against the other matter less than the actuality of the impulse to protect each one's autonomous disciplinary authority. To persuade any exegetes or theologians to participate in a coordinated interpretive endeavor, the basis for that participation must draw all concerned toward a *telos*, a good, more convincing than disciplinary autonomy. Neither discipline produces the results that the other would find compelling on its own terms.[5] So long as their interaction is a tug-of-war for authority or priority, we can hardly expect to see productive cooperation.

We won't alleviate the disciplinary stresses by constructing a new, improved metadiscourse, whose specialists would, of course, claim authority over those of the constituent fields. Rather, we need to devise a way of thinking about the interoperation of exegesis and theology (including all of theology's specializations and subfields, as well as ethics, church history, liturgics, and pastoralia) that permits us to construe each of these discourses as a salutary critical interrogation of one aspect of the integrated whole. We can gain considerable yardage toward that goal by treating these adversarial siblings as elements of the signifying practice of Christian discipleship.

Signifying Practice

The term *signifying practice* came into currency through the work of Julia Kristeva, who deployed it in the context of analyzing two ways that language functions in a text. In the first function, language cooperates with the rules, conventions, and expectations that constitute conventional usage (the "phenotext"), the structural elements that make satisfactory communication possible. The second function (the "genotext") involves the ways that communication operates beyond or athwart rule-governed patterns of expression.[6] Aural elements (timbre, sonority, speed, pitch), phonetic elements (rhyme, accent, alliteration), physiological elements (stammer, dental geography), and visual elements (the speaker's appearance, attractive scenery) all inescapably affect the auditor's uptake of meaning. In written or printed words, phenomena such as a typeface's characteristics or handwriting style, color, quality of reproduction, and page layout influence our sense of the meaning of a text. Kristeva analyzed the convergence of phenotextual and genotextual functions as the locus where all signifying takes place (even, as she allows, apart from linguistic expressions).[7]

Subsequently, the Birmingham School of cultural criticism (particularly Stuart Hall and Dick Hebdige) took up the term *signifying practice* and applied it not simply to the tension between linguistic system and specific utterances, but also to the multifarious embodied ways that people express themselves. In Hall's account, we participate in reciprocal social activities (including, but not limited to, speech and writing) in ways that affirm, amplify, and perpetuate meanings for our behavior. A particular integrated set of these words and actions constitutes a signifying practice, a complex tapestry of expression by which we assert the sorts of meaning that we and the culture around us use to define our identities.[8] Hebdige applies this cultural semiotics to the ways that nondominant social groups define themselves over against the networks of meaning that prevail in the dominant social groups.[9] Thus, gangstas, punks, goths, and various subcultures use their appearance, the sounds with which they make their presence audible, their distinct vernacular, and the gestures by which they interact with one another and with outsiders—making meaning by the ways they signify, in dress and music and speech and action.[10]

The language of signifying practices offers numerous benefits for our inquiry. First, the range of signifying practices extends far beyond the conventional verbal arguments with which exegetes and theologians conduct their daily business. Paintings, musical compositions, drama, textiles, gesture, and countless other expressive practices contribute to the semiotic economy. They communicate not as diluted approximations of verbal communication, but intensely and coherently in their own idioms.

Second, the concept of signifying practices directs our attention to the fact that all our interpretive discourses involve matters of practice, however powerfully or feebly. In this frame of reference, we do not simply "apply" our interpretive conclusions as a belated postscript to the cognitive work of textual scholarship and dogmatic reasoning. Rather, in a manner reminiscent of the Aristotelian practical syllogism, our interpretations are fulfilled in the way that our lives express our claims.

Third, this frame helps us explain how exegesis in its strictly academic, technical sense differs from the theological interpretation of Scripture, and how the conceptual work of systematic theology differs from the pastoral implementation of theological teachings.

A fourth advantage is that signifying practices are open to participation by more people than exclusively the credentialed authority figures who speak from academic or ecclesiastical offices. They also embrace the enacted exegesis and theology manifest among the saints who manage without degrees and titles.

Furthermore, when we consider exegesis and theology within the domain of signifying practices, we can better recognize the inevitable fluidity and ambiguity that attend our efforts to express the truth to which we bear witness. Where a strictly verbal account of these disciplines nurtures the illusion that we may control and police a propositionally correct definitive version of the faith, our signifying practices never attain finality, but always turn us back to discernment and judgment. We learn about exegesis and theology not solely from studying ancient languages and conciliar decrees, but also from feeding the hungry, visiting prisoners, and sheltering the beleaguered. This view might strike some as merely a liberal escape hatch by which to bootleg fuzzy "experience" into disciplined reasoning, but it is the recollection of the unanimous teaching of Scripture, the saints, and reason itself that the Truth transforms lives that acknowledge its truth.

Finally, the signifying practices to which exegesis and theology lend complementary energies may arguably point to a consummation in the church's signifying practice par excellence: the Eucharist, which is "an essential action," not "an isolated presence or merely illustrative symbol."[11]

Embodied Meaning of the Eucharist

The eucharistic consummation of theological exegesis returns us to my conjoined epigraphs. The first, de la Taille's characterization of the incarnate Word having set himself in the order of signs, serves in its original context as part of an extensive argument relative to the integrity of the Last Supper, the passion and crucifixion, and the Mass. In the present context, however, it further highlights God's eternal decision to communicate with humanity by way of embodied action, not solely by way of revealed linguistic expressions. In many and various ways, God spoke of old to Israel by the prophets;

but in these last days he has spoken to us by a Son, choosing to communicate not by word alone but by body language. As de la Taille says,

> When God willed to create the world, he created it by his Word, by his eternal locution *per quem omnia facta sunt*, as we sing in our ancient *Credo*. And when God willed to raise the world up from its ruins, he did so once more by his Word, but by his Word made flesh. . . . In his eucharistic flesh, I say, turning himself into something like a word uttered in figure by the Father, into a kind of subsisting speech, into a living and efficacious intimation of that plan of unity with which the divine intelligence is at work, in order to sum up all things in Christ, and through Christ in God.[12]

If we envision a pursuit of the truth that integrates exegesis and theology, we must account for embodied meaning not as a semiotic afterthought, the second-order application of an allegedly more real linguistic meaning. Indeed, as Pickstock has proposed, in the eucharistic recapitulation of the incarnation, we participate in the condition of the possibility of meaning.[13]

De la Taille's discourse on the "Flesh that has itself become a word, a divine oracle, in order to express the life of Christ in the members of Christ"[14] catalyzed the understanding of signifying and sacramentality that David Jones developed in a series of essays and meditations.[15] Jones proposes that the sacraments signify superabundantly the truth to which human arts, all making, point. Where we observe the impulse to forgo mere functionality in the name of useless beauty, Jones identifies an aspiration to sacramental significance:

> Let us take the names of Picasso and Joyce as world-famous practitioners of the useless within

our ever-accelerating utility-putsch: the one something of a magician and a superlatively able artist in
various disparate media, from painting to ceramics;
the other a master of the metaphoric who, in one
medium alone, commands the incantational power
of a number of media. Whereby the aural and the
ocular senses of us are confronted with a new art
form of unparalleled complexity, of signification
piled upon signification, thus producing a work of
exceptional sacramentality.[16]

In Jones's sacramental semiotics, "meaning" and "making" are inextricably intermingled, and although the eucharistic "making" uniquely effects the truth that it signifies,
nonetheless all our activity evinces some sort of relation to
the truth. To the extent that we answer the call to walk in
newness of life, to direct our energies toward participating
in the *anamnesis* (reactualization) of meaning, we can orient
our lives toward the vocation of manifesting God's glory in
all our "making," letting our light so shine before all people
that they may see our good works and give glory to God.[17]

The explanatory value of such a eucharistically shaped
life derives a warrant from God's own self-exposition in
Jesus Christ, as it is expressed in the lapidary formula in
John 1:18: "It is God the only Son, who is close to the
Father's heart, who has made him known."[18] The Johannine
Jesus emphasizes the importance of "believing in his name"
and expounds the Father's identity in lengthy monologues,
yes—but John also places a distinctive emphasis on Jesus'
role as revealer-of-the-Father, and that revelation continually foregrounds the activities by which the world can recognize the Father's identity. John depicts a Jesus who teaches
the mutual determination of knowledge and action, of belief
and works, and who instructs his followers to perpetuate
his works in order that his testimony might continue. In
typically circuitous Johannine logic, the disciples who know
Jesus, who love him and do his works, thereby know the

Father and make the Father known in the world.[19] And if we, in turn, want to take up the discipleship to which Jesus calls us in John's Gospel, we must attend to the way that the eternal Word expounded the Father's identity when he placed himself in the order of signs.

A Harmonious Order

The signifying practice of this discipleship situates both exegesis and theology (and the other theological fields) as modes of critical analysis by which we assess and refine our own participation in the economy of signification. Exegesis maintains scrupulous attention to the primary texts that shape our practice, and evaluates the soundness of our ventures in communicating God's identity relative to these precedents. Theology maintains the congruence of our sundry ventures both with the traditions to which we profess allegiance and with our other expressions of faith. Neither of these can claim systematic precedence over the other; their contributions to our clearer understanding of our vocation hang together not in a sequential or hierarchical way, but as the harmonious ordering of complementary capacities.

The harmony of this order derives not from the rigor or precision of our scholarship, not from aligning our discourses with an allegedly correct dogmatic definition, but from aligning our lives with the gifts of the Spirit: humility, patience, endurance, charity. These spiritual gifts identify the lives that bear witness to a Truth greater than our own academic prowess, our exegetical brawn. In the power of the Spirit, we who find ourselves placed in the order of signs practice a eucharistic participation in the body of Christ so that our lives, exegesis, and theology may draw near to the one who rests in the bosom of the Father, and so share in the Word's vocation to make God known.

NOTES

1. John Ferguson, trans., *Stromateis: Books 1–3*, Fathers of the Church 85 (Washington, D.C.: Catholic University Press, 1991), 279. I thank my student John Hartman for calling this text to my attention.

2. The sketch seems to have been aired in the first episode of *Rutland Weekend Television* (aired May 12, 1975, according to one online source, although the Wikipedia biographical entry for Idle asserts that the program aired only from 1973 to 1974). Idle reprised the sketch (less satisfactorily) with Dan Ackroyd on *Saturday Night Live* on April 23, 1977. The original version is included on the *Rutland Weekend Songbook*, BBC Records 1976 (BBC REB2332) record album, where I first encountered it.

3. The New Testament itself invokes genotextual features at points, but contemporary printed editions tend to suppress readers' awareness of that dimension. Consider Paul's injunction "See what large letters I make when I am writing in my own hand!" (Gal. 6:11) and his acknowledgment that his oratorical presentation is contemptible (2 Cor. 10:10).

4. The example of the Muggletonian sect also reminds interpreters that what seems stupefyingly improbable to some readers will nonetheless seem quite convincing to others, sometimes to disappointingly vast numbers of others. The Muggletonians survived from the midseventeenth century into the 1970s. In contrast, the interpreter whom I cite in chapter 3, note 4, seems not to have won many—perhaps not even any—adherents to his cause.

5. James K. A. Smith, *The Fall of Interpretation* (Downers Grove, Ill.: InterVarsity, 2000).

6. I develop this argument with much greater depth and nuance in *Making Sense of New Testament Theology* (repr. Eugene, Ore.: Wipf & Stock, 2005).

CHAPTER 1

1. The debates over what constitutes "modernism" or "modernity" and over the difference between "modern" and "postmodern" are many and unsettled. Among the important studies not cited here, see Jean-François Lyotard, "Answering the Question: What Is Postmodernism?" in *The Postmodern Condition*, trans. Régis Durand (Minneapolis: University of Minnesota Press, 1984); Jürgen Habermas, "Modernity versus Postmodernity," *New German Critique* 22 (1981): 3–14; Jürgen Habermas, *The*

Philosophical Discourse of Modernity (Cambridge, Mass.: MIT Press, 1987); Anthony Cascardi, "Genealogies of Modernism," *Philosophy and Literature* 11 (1987): 207–25; Fredric Jameson, "Postmodernism, or The Cultural Logic of Late Capitalism," *New Left Review* 146 (1984): 53–92; Frank Kermode, "The Modern," in *Modern Essays* (London: Fontana, 1971): 39–70; Matei Calinescu, *Five Faces of Modernity*, 2nd ed. (Durham, N.C.: Duke University Press, 1987); the essays in *New German Critique* 33 (1984) (including the important article by Andreas Huyssen, "Mapping the Postmodern"); and Richard J. Bernstein, ed., *Habermas and Modernity* (Cambridge, Mass.: MIT Press, 1985).

2. Joseph O'Leary, "Theology on the Brink of Modernism," *Boundary 2* 13:2/3 (1985): 145–56.

3. The social setting of the modernity I describe will have much in common with Matei Calinescu's "bourgeois modernism." See *Five Faces of Modernity*, 41–42. Calinescu notes a passage from Shakespeare that presents a particularly apt description of biblical modernists: "They say miracles are past, and we have our philosophical persons, to make modern and familiar, things supernatural and causeless" (*All's Well That Ends Well* 2.3.2).

4. Indeed, to judge by recent book titles, biblical studies seems to be vaulting directly into postmodernism, but I would hesitate to judge Edgar McKnight's *Postmodern Use of the Bible* (Nashville: Abingdon, 1988), a satisfactory first step in that direction.

5. See the distinction between scientific knowledge and narrative knowledge that Jean-François Lyotard develops in *The Postmodern Condition*, 18–31.

6. I discuss this phenomenon at greater length in "The Sign of Jonah: Getting the Big Picture (from a Fish-Eye View)," *Semeia* 51 (1990): 177–91 (chapter 7 below).

7. Barbara Herrnstein Smith discusses the notion of "non-canonical audiences" (that is, the sort of readers and interpreters who don't count when we who are interpretive professionals think about texts) in *Contingencies of Value* (Cambridge, Mass.: Harvard University Press, 1988), 25ff.

8. That is, the conservative scholar claims that she can justify believing in a bodily resurrection *on historical grounds* or concedes the necessity of bridging a hermeneutical gap (but uses more conservative historical judgment).

9. Krister Stendahl, "Biblical Theology, Contemporary," *The Interpreter's Dictionary of the Bible*, ed. George Buttrick, A–D (Nashville: Abingdon, 1962), 418ff.

10. Alan Richardson, *An Introduction to the Theology of the New Testament* (New York: SCM Press, 1958).

11. Leander Keck, "Problems of New Testament Theology," *Novum Testamentum* 7 (1964/65): 217–41.

12. Stendahl, "Biblical Theology, Contemporary," 418–32.

13. Recall Bultmann's essay on the relation of the Old and New Testaments, in which he claims that the connection between the two abides in the miscarriage of all the Old Testament promises, which miscarriage itself constitutes a promise. "Prophecy and Fulfillment," trans. James C. G. Greig, in *Essays on Old Testament Hermeneutics*, ed. Claus Westermann (Louisville: John Knox Press, 1963), 50–75.

14. Even the positions of such contemporary biblical theologians as Hartmut Gese and Peter Stuhlmacher seek only to relativize the importance of historical criticism by introducing a (subordinate) specifically theological interest. Mine is a stronger claim: we cannot helpfully reintroduce historical interpretation as a factor in biblical theology until we have utterly dethroned it.

15. Johann Philipp Gabler, "On the Proper Distinction between Biblical and Dogmatic Theology," trans. Sandys-Wunsch and Eldredge (1787), in "J. P. Gabler and the Distinction between Biblical Theology and Dogmatic Theology: Translation, Commentary, and Discussion of His Originality," *Scottish Journal of Theology* 33 (1980): 133–58.

16. William Wrede, "On the Task and Methods of 'New Testament Theology,'" trans. Robert Morgan, in *The Nature of New Testament Theology* (Naperville, Ill: Alec R. Allenson, 1973), 68–116.

17. Cf. n. 1, n. 10.

18. My reading of Gabler is greatly in the debt of Robert Morgan, "Gabler's Bicentenary," *Expository Times* 98 (1987): 164–68; and Ben Ollenburger, "Biblical Theology: Situating the Discipline," in *Understanding the Word*, ed. J. T. Butler, E. W. Conrad, and B. C. Ollenburger, JSOT Supplement Series 37 (Sheffield, England: JSOT Press, 1982): 37–62.

19. Ollenburger, "Biblical Theology," 48.

20. From the 1787 lecture, in Sandys-Wunsch and Eldredge, "J. P. Gabler," 142.

21. Remember Keck's claim: "To most men [*sic*] biblical jargon sounds like jibberish" ("Problems of New Testament Theology," 240).

22. Ben C. Ollenburger, "What Krister Stendahl 'Meant': A Normative Critique of 'Descriptive Biblical Theology,'" *Horizons in Biblical Theology* 8 (1986): 61–98.

23. See Smith, *Contingencies of Value*, for an interrogation of the possibility of necessary criteria and for a defense of contingent criteria for judgment.

24. That is, if one makes the claim, "This is a biblical theology," one authorizes the objections, "But that's not biblical at all," "But that's not what the Bible says," and so on.

25. See p. 26 above. As Richard Hays has pointed out to me, it is very interesting that he (Wrede) doesn't continue to say, "so forget about

New Testament theology," but rather calls us to *do* the historical work he advocates under the other (misleading) name.

26. I do not mean to commend summary dismissal of theological positions on the basis of casually applied labels. The names of these heresies simply refer to theological positions—based on ample scriptural testimony in each case—that have been deemed unacceptable by the dominant Christian traditions.

27. See, for example, Ernst Käsemann, "Thoughts on the Present Controversy about Scriptural Interpretation," in *New Testament Questions of Today*, trans. W. J. Montague (Philadelphia: Fortress Press, 1969), 277.

28. Of course, one could read these arguments, which I have called theological, as historical arguments that claim to see a common pattern in my more open model of interpretation and the precedents of Docetism or Gnosticism. Still, the historical interpreter cannot apply the category of "invalid" or "heretical" on the basis of these alleged common traits; that remains a distinctively theological judgment.

29. This is not to posit a discontinuity between so-called liberation theology, feminist theology, and Black theology. It would be just as wrong, however, to lump together efforts that have differing social and cultural determinants.

CHAPTER 2

1. For one example, cf. *Theology Today*'s recent historical-Jesus issue, vol. 52 (1995), with critical essays from Howard Clark Kee ("A Century of Quests for the Culturally Compatible Jesus," pp. 17–28) and Paula Fredriksen ("What You See Is What You Get: Context and Content in Current Research on the Historical Jesus," pp. 75–97).

2. John Meier alludes to this rationale in *A Marginal Jew: Rethinking the Historical Jesus*, vol. 1 (New York: Doubleday, 1991), 199, as does Marcus Borg in *Jesus in Contemporary Scholarship* (Valley Forge, Pa.: Trinity, 1994), 196. Paul Meyer, in "Faith and History Revisited," *Princeton Seminary Bulletin* 10 (1989): 75–83, has backed up his argument for the necessity of historical-critical analysis of the New Testament by contrasting his project with the "whiff of docetic unreality" he discerns in his rivals (82). My former colleague Ulrich Mauser has, in personal communication, presented the Docetism objection to my "Biblical Theology and the Problem of Modernity," *Horizons in Biblical Theology* 12 (1990): 1–19 (see chapter 1).

3. Ernst Käsemann, "Vom theologischen Recht historisch-kritischer Exegese," *Zeitschrift für Theologie und Kirche* 64:3 (1967): 281.

4. F. L. Cross and E. A. Livingstone, eds., *Oxford Dictionary of the Christian Church*, 2nd ed. (Oxford: Oxford University Press, 1974), 413; my emphasis.

5. Norbert Brox, "'Doketismus'—eine Problemanzeige," *Zeitschrift für Kirchengeschichte* 95 (1984): 301–14. All translations from Brox's article are mine.

6. Michael Slusser, "Docetism: A Historical Definition," *Second Century* 1 (1981): 163–72.

7. Translation in Alexander Roberts and James Donaldson, eds., *The Ante-Nicene Fathers* (hereafter cited as *ANF*) (repr., Grand Rapids: Eerdmans, 1989), 1:348.

8. *ANF* 1:427.

9. The relevant passages of the *Stromateis* are prudishly given in Latin in *ANF*; they are included in J. E. L. Oulton and H. Chadwick, *Alexandrian Christianity*, Library of Christian Classics 2 (Philadelphia: Westminster, 1954), 40–92.

10. *Stromateis* 3.102. This is the principal evidence that any patristic writer viewed Marcion as docetic, and even this testimony does not turn on questions of whether Jesus was fully human, but rather on whether he participated in the evil of birth. The former may be a reasonable implication from the latter, but it is not evidently in view at this point.

11. Jerry McCant argues at considerable length that the extant fragment of the *Gospel of Peter* does not suffice to confirm Serapion's judgment that it tended toward Docetism. "The Gospel of Peter: Docetism Reconsidered," *New Testament Studies* 30 (1984), 258–73. McCant's article does not devote detailed consideration to what constitutes Docetism, however, and it addresses the paucity of evidence on this point only by suggesting in a note that "much can be learned about docetism by reading anti-docetic literature" (271 n. 12) and that such texts as the *Acts of Andrew, Acts of John*, and *Acts of Peter* are "obviously" docetic. Such assumptions are hard to accept in light of the more precise historical treatment of Docetism in Brox, Slusser, and Weigandt (whose unpublished 1961 Heidelberg dissertation, *Der Doketismus im Urchristentum und in der theologischen Entwicklung des zweiten Jahrhunderts*, grounds both Slusser's and Brox's efforts). See n. 5 and n. 6 above.

Brox points out that Serapion suggests that it was the orthodox church that designated certain heretics as Docetists, whereas Hippolytus's discussion presupposes that Docetists adopted the name themselves ("Problemanzeige," 304). See n. 5 above.

12. Ernst Käsemann, *The Testament of Jesus*, trans. Gerhard Krodel (Philadelphia: Fortress Press, 1968), 9. In *The Community of the Beloved Disciple* (Ramsey, N.J.: Paulist, 1979), 116, Raymond Brown acutely points out that "Docetism" must be an anachronistic description of the Fourth Gospel.

13. Whatever import we ascribe to these characteristics of Jesus' advent, they seem clearly to point to a genuine, fleshly Jesus—especially in this context.

14. Slusser, "Docetism: A Historical Definition," 162.

15. Brox, "Problemanzeige," 309. This definition summarizes Brox's more detailed point that "[classical Docetism] is not the christology that is called 'Docetism' today, unless one wants to see the connection of the savior and his particular body in this very difficult text as quite ephemeral, superficial, only apparent and purely functional (shielding other beings from the sight of him, which they would not be able to withstand). Yet it seems that great emphasis is laid on the reality and solidity of his corporeality; and it seems that his connection or 'clothing' with a body is thought a real, actual quality, which is not what the contemporary concept of 'Docetism' means" (305).

16. This is all the more true since historical criticism is never as "neutral" as it would like to be (or as I have allowed herein). Historical inquiry always participates in one or another agenda, which is usually hidden behind a façade of objectivity.

17. Käsemann, "Vom theologischen Recht," 281.

18. Ernst Käsemann, *New Testament Questions of Today*, trans. W. J. Montague (London: SCM; Philadelphia: Fortress Press, 1969). "The total of all the individual testimonies is not the Gospel. Otherwise, the Bible would be the book which fell from heaven and Docetism would determine our concept of revelation" (9); and (in a context in which Käsemann invokes Docetism within a few sentences): "A canon in which there were not some unevangelical doctrine could only be a book fallen directly from heaven" (278).

19. Ibid., 277.

20. Cf. Käsemann, "Vom theologischen Recht": "the naïveté of a docetic enthusiasm" (270, my translation).

21. Ernst Käsemann, *Essays on New Testament Themes*, trans. W. J. Montague (London: SCM, 1964; Philadelphia: Fortress Press, 1982), 32.

22. Käsemann, "Vom theologischen Recht," 270.

23. Ibid., 280.

24. Brox, "Problemanzeige," esp. 300–303.

25. Käsemann, *New Testament Questions of Today*, 277. Käsemann uses the Jacob/Esau metaphor in quite a number of his essays; it seems to have been a rhetorical reference point for his methodological and theological reflections.

26. Käsemann, *Essays on New Testament Themes*, 45–46.

27. Käsemann, "Vom theologischen Recht," 270–71. This interest also motivates arguments in, for example, Christopher Bryan, "The Preachers and the Critics," *Anglican Theological Review* 74 (1992): 37–53. Bryan upholds the believer's responsibility to pursue honestly any critical question about the Bible (41) and accuses conservative interpreters of intellectual dishonesty and of "running away from perfectly evident questions" (43).

28. There is a certain irony in Käsemann, the defender of the faith of historical criticism, eliding the (historical) differences between ancient Docetists and his own contemporary opponents.

29. The discussion of whether theology is *wissenschaftliche* (scientific) seems to have been joined on every side recently; cf. Hans Frei, "Theology in the University: The Case of Berlin, 1810," in *Types of Christian Theology*, ed. George Hunsinger and William C. Placher (New Haven: Yale University Press, 1992), 95–116; and David Kelsey, *Between Athens and Berlin* (Grand Rapids: Eerdmans, 1993). One interesting and overlooked artifact of biblical criticism's place in this discussion is William Wrede, "Biblische Kritik und theologisches Studium," in *Vorträge und Studien* (Tübingen, Germany: Mohr [Siebeck], 1907), 40–63.

30. Since the literature that exposes the limitations of conventional historical criticism is gradually expanding, I will not undertake a comprehensive critique here; for more detail, cf., among others, A. K. M. Adam, *What Is Postmodern Biblical Criticism?* (Minneapolis: Fortress Press, 1995); chapters 1 and 7 in this volume; James Dawsey, "The Lost Front Door into Scripture: Carlos Mesters, Latin American Liberation Theology, and the Church Fathers," *Anglican Theological Review* 72 (1990): 292–305; Stanley Hauerwas and D. Stephen Long, "Interpreting the Bible as a Political Act," *Religion and Intellectual Life* 6:3/4 (1989): 134–42; Andrew Louth, *Discerning the Mystery* (Oxford: Clarendon, 1983); The Bible and Culture Collective, *The Postmodern Bible* (New Haven: Yale University Press, 1995); and, of course, Walter Wink, *The Bible in Human Transformation* (Philadelphia: Fortress Press, 1973).

31. See the testimony in Käsemann's moving "What I Have Unlearned in Fifty Years as a German Theologian," *Currents in Theology and Mission* 15 (1988): 325–35. This is perhaps the suitable place for me to express my deep appreciation for much that Käsemann stands for; his frankness and courage are powerful models for biblical scholars to emulate. My dispute here is with Käsemann's argument, not with the numerous commendable dimensions of his scholarship.

32. Albert Schweitzer, *The Quest of the Historical Jesus* (Minneapolis: Fortress Press, 2001).

33. Need one stress the work of the Jesus Seminar as an example of ill-founded confidence in historians' capacity to tell the world the truth about Jesus?

34. Robert M. Grant and David Tracy, *A Short History of the Interpretation of the Bible*, 2nd ed. (Minneapolis: Fortress Press, 1984); John Rogerson, Christopher Rowland, and Barnabas Lindars, *The Study and Use of the Bible*, History of Christian Theology 2 (Grand Rapids: Marshall Pickering/ Eerdmans, 1988); and Robert Morgan and John Barton, *Biblical Interpretation*, rev. ed. (Oxford: Oxford University Press, 1989). Morgan and Barton, it should be noted, do not fit into the pattern of a "triumphal procession of historical criticism"; they insightfully allow that the tradition of academic historical criticism has not discovered the one theologically and intellectually correct mode of interpretation. They do, however, anchor legitimate

interpretation in a "rational" defense of historical-critical reconstruction of the original meaning of a text.

CHAPTER 3

1. Elisabeth Schüssler Fiorenza came first, presenting "The Ethics of Interpretation: Decentering Biblical Scholarship," *Journal of Biblical Literature* 107 (1988): 3–17, her presidential address to the Society of Biblical Literature. Stephen Fowl presented a promissory essay, "The Ethics of Interpretation, or What's Left Over after the Elimination of Meaning?" which was in part a response to Schüssler Fiorenza's address. Fowl's essay appeared first in the *SBL 1988 Seminar Papers*, ed. David J. Lull (Atlanta: Scholars Press, 1988), 69–81, then was revised and reprinted in *The Bible in Three Dimensions*, ed. David Clines, Stephen Fowl, and Stanley Porter (Sheffield: JSOT Press, 1990), 379–98. Fowl followed up this promissory note in collaboration with L. Gregory Jones, in *Reading in Communion: Scripture and Ethics in Christian Life* (Grand Rapids: Eerdmans, 1991). His "Texts Don't Have Ideologies," *Biblical Interpretation* 3 (1995): 15–34, also bears on the issues I examine here. For my sketch of some of the ways his position informs mine, see "Matthew's Readers, Ideology, and Power," *SBL 1994 Seminar Papers*, ed. Eugene H. Lovering Jr. (Atlanta: Scholars Press, 1994), 435–49 (chapter 4, below); cf. also Margaret B. Adam, "This Is My Story, This Is My Song" in *Escaping Eden*, ed. Harold C. Washington, Susan Lochrie Graham, and Pamela Thimmes (Sheffield, England: Sheffield Academic Press, 1998), 218-32. Most recently, Daniel Patte has produced an account of "androcritical multidimensional exegesis" in *Ethics of Biblical Interpretation* (Minneapolis: Fortress Press, 1995). Patte engages Schüssler Fiorenza's position but (oddly) omits any reference to Fowl, though Fowl's original "Ethics of Interpretation" paper was read for a session of the SBL Semiotics and Exegesis Section that Patte chaired.

2. The best-known expositions of the social character of interpretation and criticism are Stanley Fish's *Is There a Text in This Class?* (Cambridge, Mass.: Harvard University Press, 1979); and *Doing What Comes Naturally* (Durham, N.C.: Duke University Press, 1989). But two works illuminate much that Fish's flair overshadows: Barbara Herrnstein Smith, *Contingencies of Value* (Cambridge, Mass.: Harvard University Press, 1988); and Tony Bennett, "Texts in History: The Determinations of Readings and Their Texts," in *Post-Structuralism and the Question of History* (Cambridge: Cambridge University Press, 1987), 63–81. I will hereafter adopt Bennett's term *reading formations* for conjunctions of readers, audiences, texts, and social circumstances.

3. Fowl adumbrates a similar position in "The Ethics of Interpretation" and (esp. with Jones) in *Reading in Communion*. Fowl refers to

interpreters who undertake their readings on the basis of a self-conscious, critical relation to their reading formations as "communal interpreters." His works tend to emphasize a community not only of interpretive interests, but also of many concrete aspects of daily life. This emphasis contrasts sharply with Stanley Fish's "communities of interpretation" (*Is There a Text in This Class?*), which often appear rather abstract, apparently amounting to little more than the set of people who assent to a particular interpretation at a particular moment. While my account of the social dimensions of reading falls between these two accounts—some reading formations depend less on shared *daily life* than on a sense of *mutual accountability*—my socially constituted interpreters are very much more Fowl's than Fish's.

4. I could, however, recognize that it is appropriate for "tabloid" people to generate and approve of such interpretations—while at the same time maintaining that there are important reasons to stretch one's imagination in other ways that I would characterize as more "responsible." Lee Perry, author of a variety of works that argue for reading the New Testament as the repository of a pre-Christian Celtic religion, its calendars, physics, and mathematics, has acknowledged that some may view his work as a "two-headed frog story" (personal communication). See his books *The Holy Grail: Source of the Ancient Science and Spirituality of the Circling Cosmos* (Cumming, Ga.: Saoirse Cainte Press, 1993) and *The Holy Grail: Cosmos of the Bible* (New York: Philosophical Library, 1991) for an illustration of an interpretation that is far from arbitrary but will never persuade a scholarly audience.

5. Jean-François Lyotard discusses this phenomenon in its broader philosophical ethical context in *The Differend: Phrases in Dispute*, trans. Georges Van Den Abbeele, Theory and History of Literature 46 (Minneapolis: University of Minnesota Press, 1988). Lyotard differentiates a "differend" from a "litigation" because the former "case cannot be equitably resolved for lack of a rule of judgment applicable to both arguments" (xi), whereas the latter case can satisfactorily be adjudicated according to conventional norms.

6. In "The Sign of Jonah: Getting the Big Picture (from a Fish-Eye View)," *Semeia* 51 (1990): 177–91, I discuss this phenomenon with respect to Fish's analysis of "communities of interpretation." See chapter 7.

7. This is one serious problem with Daniel Patte's *Ethics of Biblical Intepretation* (see note 1), which in many other respects is a salutary admission that interpretive legitimacy does not depend on an academic imprimatur. Patte recognizes the problem of the academic hermeneutical hegemony but believes that his vocation as a "critical" exegete warrants his judging the validity of "ordinary readings." The very language in which he couches these characterizations points to serious problems with his position.

8. The antivivisection and animal-rights movements provide useful examples of the ethical criticism of scientific research. While there is widespread revulsion at the ways animals are treated in some experiments,

the goal of "furthering scientific knowledge" insulates scientists from the full force of ethical disapprobation, just as the goal of "furthering scientific knowledge" shields biblical scholars from theological and ethical criticism.

CHAPTER 4

1. Fred Burnett, "Exposing the Anti-Jewish Ideology of Matthew's Implied Author: The Characterization of God as Father," *Semeia* 59 (1993): 156.

2. Stephen Fowl, "Texts Don't Have Ideologies," *Biblical Interpretation* 3 (1995): 1–34.

3. Cf. Jeffrey Stout, "What Is the Meaning of a Text?" in *New Literary History* 14 (1982): 1–12. Fowl applies Stout's argument in his "The Ethics of Interpretation, or What's Left Over after the Elimination of Meaning?" in *The Bible in Three Dimensions*, ed. David J. A. Clines, Stephen E. Fowl, and Stanley Porter (Sheffield: JSOT Press, 1990), 379–98. The same principle rules out Patte's contention that texts harbor encoded "intentions"; the intentions aren't there until and unless we are looking for them.

4. Fowl, "Texts Don't Have Ideologies," 22.

5. While such endeavors are familiar in the biblical disciplines, their familiarity does not warrant the conclusion that they are sound. Biblical scholars are lamentably prone to the intellectual error of transforming Monday's speculation into Tuesday's consensus into Wednesday's "assured results of scholarly study" into Thursday's "fact"—with no additional evidence, and often in the teeth of learned opposition.

6. Fowl, "Texts Don't Have Ideologies," 26.

7. Daniel Defoe, "The Shortest-Way with the Dissenters," in *Eighteenth-Century English Literature*, ed. Geoffrey Tillotson, Paul Fusell Jr., and Marshall Waingrow (New York: Harcourt, Brace & World, 1969), 240.

8. Lee Perry, *The Holy Grail: Source of the Ancient Science and Spirituality of the Circling Cosmos* (Cumming, Ga.: Saoirse Cainte Press, 1993).

9. Tony Bennett, "Texts in History: The Determinations of Readings and Their Texts," in *Post-Structuralism and the Question of History*, ed. Derek Attridge, Geoff Bennington, and Robert Young (Cambridge: Cambridge University Press, 1987), 63–81. Fred Burnett addresses the complexity of "reading formations" by expanding "the text" until it embraces "the rules and conventions which are immanent in our reading practices, practices which *form* both the object about which we speak and ourselves" (Burnett, "Exposing the Anti-Jewish Ideology," 158). I heartily endorse his attention to the practices that form our readings and ourselves, but I balk at conflating the various dimensions of interpretive practices under the label *the text*. If I have no other reason, I fear the risk of important slippage between (on one hand) "the text" that my colleagues and I produce and participate in and (on the other hand) "the text" as the graphic provoca-

tion of our interpretations. The two "texts" are clearly intertwined, but I hesitate to assume they are identical.

10. One might, I suppose, contend that Matthew argues self-destructively against a Judaism that he himself espouses; but I am not aware that anyone takes this position. Consider the compelling arguments by such critics as Fred Burnett, "Exposing the Anti-Jewish Ideology"; Daniel Patte, "Anti-Semitism in the New Testament: Confronting the Dark Side of Paul's and Matthew's Teaching," *Chicago Theological Seminary Register* 78 (1988): 31–52; and Jon Levenson, "Is There a Counterpart in the Hebrew Bible to New Testament Antisemitism?" *Journal of Ecumenical Studies* 22:2 (1985): 242–60. Certainly, these presuppose that Matthew is arguing over against a Judaism from which he is already separate.

11. Burnett, "Exposing the Anti-Jewish Ideology," 155.

12. The position is especially associated with Jacob Neusner's innumerable and instructive writings, but see also Gabriele Boccaccini, *Middle Judaism: Jewish Thought, 300 B.C.E. to 200 C.E.* (Minneapolis: Fortress Press, 1991); Anthony Saldarini, *Pharisees, Scribes, and Sadducees in Palestinian Society* (Wilmington, Del.: Michael Glazier, 1988); and Wayne Meeks, "Breaking Away: Three New Testament Pictures of Christianity's Separation from the Jewish Communities," in *"To See Ourselves as Others See Us": Christians, Jews, "Others" in Late Antiquity*, ed. Jacob Neusner and Ernst S. Frerichs (Chico, Calif.: Scholars Press, 1985), 93–115.

13. Jacob Neusner's introduction to *Judaisms and Their Messiahs* (Cambridge: Cambridge University Press, 1987) stresses this point, and the contents of the volume reflect it. Essays by Kee and MacRae on messianism and the Gospels appear side by side with essays by Stone, Talmon, Goldstein, and Nickelsburg on messianism in other Judaisms.

14. Scot McKnight, "A Loyal Critic: Matthew's Polemic with Judaism in Theological Perspective," in *Anti-Semitism in Early Christianity*, ed. Craig A. Evans and Donald A. Hagner (Minneapolis: Fortress Press, 1993), 55–79; 61.

15. Bruce Chilton exemplifies the historical problem when he argues on the one hand that Matthew brands "Jews" as liars and murderers, adding that this "is the most prejudicial charge in all of the Gospels," then stresses that "Jesus and his movement were essentially Judaic" and that Matthew is "the best illustration of the conscious emergence" of Christian discipleship as "a systematic alternative to the rabbinic Judaism that emerged after 70 CE." Chilton, "Jesus and the Question of Anti-Semitism," *Anti-Semitism and Early Christianity*, ed. Craig A. Evans and Donald Hagner (Minneapolis: Fortress Press, 1993), 40, 42. Likewise, Daniel Patte argues both that "Matthew was written after the separation of Christianity from Judaism" and that "Matthew still views the Christian faith as a form of Judaism" ("Anti-Semitism in the New Testament," 49, 50).

16. Patte, "Anti-Semitism in the New Testament," 50–51.

17. James Charlesworth, "'Jews,' 'Pagans,' and 'Christians' in Antiquity and Our Search for 'The Next Step,'" *Explorations* 8:1 (1994): 1.

18. Bruce J. Malina and Richard L. Rohrbaugh, *Social-Science Commentary on the Synoptic Gospels* (Minneapolis: Fortress Press, 1992), 168–69.

19. This is most obvious in Martin Bormann's memo, which states flatly, "National Socialism and Christian concepts are incompatible." Quoted in George L. Mosse, *Nazi Culture* (repr., New York: Schocken, 1988), 244.

20. Ludwig Müller, *Deutsche Gottesworte Aus der Bergpredigt verdeutscht* (Weimar/Thüringen: Verlag Deutsche Christen, 1936). The title is misleading; Müller germanizes not only the Sermon on the Mount, but also other miscellaneous sayings from the New Testament and conventional Christian piety.

21. "Wenn du betest, hüte dich vor aller Heuchelei. Wer in der Öffentlichkeit nur deshalb betest, weil er vor den Leuten fromm erscheinen will, der ist ein Heuchler; und alles heuchlerische Beten ist vor Gott und Menschen ein Greuel" (Müller, *Deutsche Gottesworte*, 19). "When you pray, guard yourself against hypocrisy. Whoever prays in public just because he wants to appear pious before society is a hypocrite, and all hypocritical prayer is an abomination before God and people."

22. Cf. Émile C. Fabre, *God's Underground: CIMADE 1939–1945*, trans. William and Patricia Nottingham (St. Louis: Bethany, 1970), passim. Lest I here be understood to be romantically positing a univocally cordial relation between French Christian Resistance and Judaism, be it observed that Témoignage Chrétien took a pro-Arab stance in the Yom Kippur War. Cf. Franklin H. Littell, *The Crucifixion of the Jews*, Reprints of Scholarly Excellence (Macon, Ga.: Mercer University Press, 1986), 85.

23. Susan Zuccotti, *The Holocaust, the French, and the Jews* (New York: Basic Books, 1993), 231.

24. One difficulty with Patte's reading is that his dedication to resisting anti-Judaism seems to leave little reason for anyone to be a Christian. Just as early-twentieth-century Christian interpretations of Judaism "raise the question of how a member of the species *homo sapiens* could ever be attracted to such a degraded and unhappy way of life" (Levenson, "Is There a Counterpart . . .?" 243), so contemporary Christian accounts of Judaism raise the question of whether there is any justification for an ethically sensitive *Homo sapiens* confessing Jesus as the Christ. We do not solve the problem of culture's anti-Judaism by demeaning Christian faith; we do not advance dialogue by suggesting that it is improper for Christians to think they have any compelling reason to adhere to faith in Jesus rather than obedience to Torah.

CHAPTER 5

1. E. D. Hirsch, *Validity in Interpretation* (New Haven: Yale University Press, 1967); and Hirsch, "Three Dimensions of Hermeneutics," in *The Aims of Interpretation* (Chicago: University of Chicago Press, 1976).

2. Anthony C. Thiselton, *New Horizons in Hermeneutics: The Theory and Practice of Transforming Biblical Reading* (London: HarperCollins; Grand Rapids: Zondervan, 1992); Francis Watson, *Text, Church, and World: Biblical Interpretation in Theological Perspective* (Grand Rapids: Eerdmans, 1994; Edinburgh: T&T Clark, 1994); Francis Watson, *Text and Truth: Redefining Biblical Theology* (Grand Rapids: Eerdmans; Edinburgh: T&T Clark, 1997); Kevin J. Vanhoozer, *Is There a Meaning in This Text? The Bible, the Reader, and the Morality of Biblical Knowledge* (Leicester, England: Apollos; Grand Rapids: Zondervan, 1998); and Kevin J. Vanhoozer, "Body Piercing, the Natural Sense, and the Task of Theological Interpretation: A Hermeneutical Homily on John 19.34," *Ex auditu* 16 (2000): 1–29.

3. My summary of the trinitarian case for integral hermeneutics grossly oversimplifies—but does not, I think, parody—Kevin Vanhoozer's arguments (*Is There a Meaning in This Text?* 455–57).

4. Daniel Patte, *Ethics of Biblical Interpretation: A Reevaluation* (Louisville: Westminster John Knox, 1995); Patte, *Discipleship according to the Sermon on the Mount: Four Legitimate Readings, Four Plausible Views of Discipleship, and Their Relative Values* (Valley Forge, Pa.: Trinity, 1996); Charles H. Cosgrove, *Elusive Israel: The Puzzle of Election in Romans* (Louisville: Westminster John Knox, 1997); Cosgrove, *Appealing to Scripture in Moral Debate: Five Hermeneutical Rules* (Grand Rapids: Eerdmans, 2002), 154–80; James K. A. Smith, *The Fall of Interpretation: Philosophical Foundations for a Creational Hermeneutic* (Downers Grove, Ill.: InterVarsity, 2000); Stephen Fowl, *Engaging Scripture: A Model for Theological Interpretation* (Oxford: Basil Blackwell, 1999); Stephen Fowl and L. Gregory Jones, *Reading in Communion: Scripture and Ethics in Christian Life* (Grand Rapids: Eerdmans, 1991); A. K. M. Adam, "The Future of Our Allusions," *Society of Biblical Literature Seminar Papers* 31 (1992): 5–13; Adam, *Making Sense of New Testament Theology: "Modern" Problems and Prospects*, Studies in American Biblical Hermeneutics 11 (Macon, Ga.: Mercer University Press, 1995); Adam, "The Sign of Jonah: Getting the Big Picture (from a Fish-Eye View)," *Semeia* 51 (1990): 177–91 (see chapter 7 below); Adam, "Twisting to Destruction: A Memorandum on the Ethics of Interpretation," *Perspectives in Religious Studies* 23 (1996): 215–22 (see chapter 3 above); Adam, *What Is Postmodern Biblical Criticism?* (Minneapolis: Fortress Press, 1995); Elisabeth Schüssler Fiorenza, "The Ethics of Biblical Interpretation: Decentering Biblical Scholarship," *Journal of Biblical Literature* 107 (1988): 3–17; Schüssler Fiorenza, *Rhetoric and Ethic: The Politics of Biblical Studies* (Minneapolis: Fortress Press, 1999). Two other scholars are Trevor George Hunsberger Bechtel,

"How to Eat Your Bible: Performance and Understanding for Mennonites," *Conrad Grebel Review* 21:2 (Spring 2003): 81–87; and Margaret B. Adam, "'This Is My Story, This Is My Song . . .': A Feminist Claim on Scripture, Ideology, and Interpretation," in *Escaping Eden*, ed. Harold C. Washington, Susan Lochrie Graham, and Pamela Thimmes (Sheffield, England: Sheffield Academic Press, 1998), 218–32.

5. Hans Dieter Betz, *The Sermon on the Mount: A Commentary on the Sermon on the Mount*, Hermeneia (Minneapolis: Fortress Press, 1995); Donald A. Carson, *The Sermon on the Mount: An Evangelical Exposition of Matthew 5–7* (Grand Rapids: Baker, 1978); Donald A. Carson, *Jesus' Sermon on the Mount and His Confrontation with the World: An Exposition of Matthew 5–10* (Toronto: Global Christian Publishers, 1999); Amy-Jill Levine, "Matthean Jesus, Biblical Law, and Hemorrhaging Woman," in *Treasures Old and New: Recent Contributions to Matthean Studies*, ed. D. R. Bauer and M. A. Powell, Symposium Series 1 (Atlanta: Scholars Press, 1996), 379–97; Amy-Jill Levine, "Anti-Judaism and the Gospel of Matthew," in *Anti-Judaism and the Gospels*, ed. William R. Farmer (Valley Forge, Pa.: Trinity, 1999), 9–36; Levine, "Matthew's Advice to a Divided Readership," in *The Gospel of Matthew in Current Study: Studies in Memory of William G. Thompson, S.J.*, ed. David E. Aune (Grand Rapids: Eerdmans, 2001), 22–41.

6. On Schüssler Fiorenza's notion of kyriarchy, see her book *Rhetoric and Ethic*, ix and passim.

CHAPTER 6

1. Charles M. Sheldon, *In His Steps* (Nashville: Broadman, n.d.).

2. The "next to the Bible" claim is trotted out for many books; my copy of *In His Steps* makes the same claim. Sheldon neglected to copyright his book, so innumerable inexpensive copies rolled from the presses of opportunistic publishers, making it extremely difficult to come up with even a rough count of the number of copies this book sold.

3. Michael G. Cartwright, "*The Once and Future Church* Revisited," in *Embodied Holiness: Toward a Corporate Theology of Spiritual Growth*, ed. Samuel M. Powell and Michael E. Lodahl (Downers Grove, Ill.: InterVarsity Press, 1999), 115–44.

4. Ibid., 121.

5. Cartwright observes that the First Church congregation seems curiously far off from the Bible they claim to follow.

6. Elizabeth Castelli, *Imitating Paul: A Discourse of Power* (Louisville: Westminster John Knox, 1991), 57.

7. Castelli, *Imitating Paul*, 47, drawing particularly on Michel Foucault's "The Subject and Power," in *Michel Foucault: Beyond Structuralism and Hermeneutics*, ed. Hubert Dreyfus and Paul Rabinow (Chicago: University of Chicago Press, 1982), 208–26.

8. 1 Thess. 1:6 ("of us and of the Lord"); 1 Thess. 2:14 ("You . . . became imitators of the churches of God . . . in Judea"); and Phil. 3:17 ("Be co-imitators [*summimētai*] of me"). Castelli includes a short consideration of Gal 4:12 ("Become as I [am]"), which, she argues, functions in the same way as the explicit use of *mimētai*. Castelli, *Imitating Paul*, 115–16.

9. Castelli, *Imitating Paul*, 117.

10. At least, one might expect to find such a Christianity-improved-without-Jesus only in the remaindered sensationalism of John Spong and his ilk.

11. In "Do This: A Eucharistic Self," David Ford presents an argument complementary to mine. Where I stress the practice of the imitation of Christ, he emphasizes the Eucharist as the focus of our transformation into the image of God. His essay appears as chapter 6 of *Self and Salvation: Being Transformed* (Cambridge: Cambridge University Press, 1999), 137–65. Ford offers a longer and deeper exploration of our intertwined topics than appears here, and it would be an ideal second helping to any who are intrigued by the taste of radical orthodox theology offered in this article. Even more intensely illuminating are the works associated with the Radical Orthodox theologians: Graham Ward, *Barth, Derrida, and the Language of Theology* (Cambridge: Cambridge University Press, 1995); Catherine Pickstock, *After Writing: On the Liturgical Consummation of Philosophy* (Oxford: Blackwell, 1998); John Milbank, *Theology and Social Theory: Beyond Secular Reason* (Oxford: Blackwell, 1990); and esp. John Milbank, Catherine Pickstock, and Graham Ward, eds., *Radical Orthodoxy: A New Theology* (London: Routledge, 1999).

12. Aristotle, *Metaphysics* 1005b–1006a, trans. Hugh Tredennick, Loeb Classical Library (Cambridge, Mass.: Harvard University Press, 1933).

13. Due credit should be given to Heraclitus's successor Cratylus, who argued that one cannot do so *once* (*Metaphysics* 1010a).

14. Jean-François Lyotard, *The Postmodern Condition*, trans. Geoff Bennington and Brian Massumi, Theory and History of Literature 10 (Minneapolis: University of Minnesota Press, 1979), 44–47, 54–67.

15. Lyotard, "Answering the Question: What Is Postmodernism?" in ibid., 82.

16. For a profound meditation on this topic, see Gilles Deleuze's densely argued *Difference and Repetition*, trans. Paul Patton (New York: Columbia University Press, 1994), whose influence saturates these pages. Recent process thought has devoted special attention to Deluze in conjunction with his study of Whitehead and Bergson; Roland Faber deals with such issues in "Toward a Hermeneutics of the Unique" (conference paper, Relational Hermeneutics in a Fractured World, Center for Process Studies, Claremont, Calif., February 2000).

17. Derrida returns to the theme of "Signature Event Context" frequently. The following paragraphs lean most specifically on the essays

compiled into *Limited Inc* (Evanston, Ill.: Northwestern University Press, 1988), but a diligent reader will want to consult "Ulysses Gramophone: Hear Say Yes in Joyce," trans. Tina Kendall and Shari Benstock, in *Jacques Derrida: Acts of Literature*, ed. Derek Attridge (New York: Routledge, 1992), 256–309; and *The Post Card: From Socrates to Freud and Beyond*, trans. Alan Bass (Chicago: University of Chicago Press, 1987).

18. For a helpful introduction to Luce Irigaray, see Faith Kirkham Hawkins's essay, "Irigaray," in *Handbook of Postmodern Biblical Interpretation*, ed. A. K. M. Adam (St. Louis: Chalice, 2000), 131–37, which has helped inform the following paragraphs. Likewise instructive are Grace Jantzen's introduction to Irigaray's "Equal to Whom?" (an ambivalent response to Elisabeth Schüssler Fiorenza's *In Memory of Her*), in *The Postmodern God*, ed. Graham Ward (Oxford: Blackwell, 1997), 198–213; and Margaret Whitford's *Luce Irigaray: Philosophy in the Feminine* (London: Routledge, 1991).

19. Michel de Certeau, "Reading as Poaching," in *The Practice of Everyday Life*, trans. Steven Rendall (Berkeley: University of California Press, 1984), 165–76 (on interpretation); and Certeau, "How Is Christianity Thinkable Today?" in *The Postmodern God*, 142–55 (on theology). For two admirable introductions, see Frederick Bauerschmidt's introduction to the Certeau material in *The Postmodern God* (135–41); and Vincent J. Miller, "Certeau," in *Handbook of Postmodern Biblical Interpretation*, 42–48.

20. Certeau, "How Is Christianity Thinkable Today?" 142.

21. For a similar point, developed at greater length, see Jon L. Berquist, *Incarnation*, Understanding Biblical Themes (St. Louis: Chalice, 1999), esp. 146–50.

22. The past will not give over its otherness, even to the most forceful interpretations. Our continual efforts to make contact with and re-present the past do not exhaust or assimilate the past to our purposes. Rather, history writing is always "heterological," not only in that it writes about the (past) Other, but also inasmuch as the Other about which it writes remains Other, accessible to the *next* historiographer's version of the past.

23. Certeau, "How Is Christianity Thinkable Today?" 146.

24. Perhaps at the end, all of these accounts of identity and difference themselves exemplify a differential repetition of Kierkegaard. For all the attention he has received in recent theological discourse, we have by no means come to the end of all our exploring of his invitation to repetition. Though interpretations of Kierkegaard abound, at least one current of criticism depicts a Kierkegaard whose concept of repetition prefigures, and haunts, a postmodern imitation of *Repetition*: Søren Kierkegaard, *Fear and Trembling/Repetition*, ed. and trans. Howard V. Hong and Edna H. Hong (Princeton: Princeton University Press, 1983). For a thin slice of the vast literature, I invoke John D. Caputo, *Radical Hermeneutics* (Bloomington: Indiana University Press, 1987); John Milbank, "The Sublime in Kierkegaard," in *Post-secular Philosophy*, ed. Philip Blond (London: Rout-

ledge, 1998), 131–56; Arne Melberg, "*Repetition* (in the Kierkegaardian Sense of the Term)," *Diacritics* 20:3 (1990): 71–87; and Jacques Derrida, *The Gift of Death*, trans. David Wills (Chicago: University of Chicago Press, 1995).

25. John Milbank, "The Name of Jesus," in *The Word Made Strange* (Oxford: Blackwell, 1997), 152. Milbank presses a distinction between imitation (an unfavorable mode in which a transcendent Other constitutes an unchanging model for our attempts at reproduction) and repetition (an appropriate mode in which the repeated practice itself provides the criterion of continuity). Milbank's resistance to the premise of a "real point of origination" should be read in conjunction with his identification of Jesus as "the founder of a new or renewed law and community" and his resistance to an individualism that risks citing Jesus as an originary instance of a principle or idea that preceded him. Instead, Milbank espouses an ecclesiocentric iteration of Jesus' identity.

26. Stephen Fowl makes a very similar point with special regard to Philippians in "Christology and Ethics in Philippians 2:5–11," in *Where Christology Began*, ed. R. P. Martin and Brian Dodd (Louisville: Westminster John Knox, 1998), 140–53, 148.

27. Indeed, it may be that the only way in which two recitations of the creed coincide lies in the agreed-upon context with reference to which my Peruvian sisters, my Japanese brothers, and I all recite words we affirm to have been handed down to us (with the mediation of generations of the saints) from the Nicene and Constantinopolitan Councils.

28. Church of England, *Thirty-Nine Articles of Religion*, art. 19, "Of the Church."

29. Fowl, "Christology and Ethics," 149.

30. "The question of whether human thinking attains to objective truth is not a question of theory, but is a *practical* question. One must prove the truth, that is, the reality and power, the this-sidedness of one's thinking, in practice. The dispute over the reality or non-reality of thinking that is isolated from practice is a purely *scholastic* question." Karl Marx, "Theses on Feuerbach," Thesis II, in *The Marx-Engels Reader*, 2nd ed. (New York: W. W. Norton & Co., 1978), 144.

CHAPTER 7

1. Stanley Fish, *Is There a Text in This Class?* (Cambridge, Mass.: Harvard University Press, 1980), 303–71; and Frank Kermode, *The Art of Telling* (Cambridge, Mass.: Harvard University Press, 1983), 156–84.

2. Michael LaFargue, *Language and Gnosis*, Harvard Dissertations in Religion 18 (Philadelphia: Fortress Press, 1985), 4–8 and passim. This type of interpretation might be related to Peter Stuhlmacher's "hermeneutics of consent," which according to Stuhlmacher rests on "scientific" grounds.

Stuhlmacher, *Historical Criticism and the Theological Interpretation of Scripture*, trans. Roy A. Harrisville (Philadelphia: Fortress Press, 1977), 83–91.

3. Kermode, *Art of Telling*, 165.

4. Gustavo Perez-Firmat, "Interpretive Assumptions and Interpreted Texts: On a Poem by Stanley Fish," *Essays in Literature* 9 (1984): 145–52; Walter A. Davis, "The Fisher King: *Wille zur Macht* in Baltimore," *Critical Inquiry* 10 (1984): 668–94; Gerald Graff, "Interpretation on Tlön: A Response to Stanley Fish," *New Literary History* 17 (1985): 109–17.

5. Robert Scholes, *Textual Power* (New Haven: Yale University Press, 1985), 149–65; and Stanley Fish, "Fear of Fish: A Reply to Walter Davis," *Critical Inquiry* 10 (1984): 695–703.

6. Fish suggests that interpretation necessarily involves the ascription of intention (whether to the author, the Holy Spirit, or some other agent held responsible for the meaning of the text), so that outlandish textual exercises must either ascribe intention ('Shakespeare intended *Hamlet* to correspond to Javanese astrology') or forfeit the description 'interpretation.' Fish, "Working on the Chain Gang: Interpretation in the Law and in Literary Criticism," *Critical Inquiry* 9 (1982): 201–16; and Fish, "Wrong Again," *Texas Law Review* 62 (1983): 299–316.

7. Fish, *Is There a Text in This Class?* vii; and Fish, "Resistance and Independence: A Reply to Gerald Graff," *New Literary History* 17 (1985): 119–27.

8. For a more detailed description of Fish's work, see Stephen D. Moore, "Negative Hermeneutics, Insubstantial Texts: Stanley Fish and the Biblical Interpreter," *Journal of the American Academy of Religion* 54 (1986): 707–19. See also Jeffrey Stout's important essay, "What Is the Meaning of a Text?" *New Literary History* 13 (1982): 1–12.

9. I use the word *productive* here assuming a polemical or apologetic context; obviously a given reader's attack upon an unsympathetic critic may be productive within that reader's community, building a sense that the blinkered Philistine has been bested. But if readers are concerned to persuade and be understood by others outside their communities, they will strategically presuppose only such commitments and interests as they hold in common with their intended audience. Strictly speaking, of course, one can never interpret texts on the basis of any commitments other than one's own. This passage simply reflects my own interest in persuading others that my interpretive claims are justified.

10. Justin, *Dialogue with Trypho* 107, in *The Ante-Nicene Fathers*, ed. Alexander Roberts and James Donaldson, 1 (Buffalo: Christian Literature Publishing, 1885), 194–270, esp. 252–53; Cyprian, *Treatise XII*, "Three Books of Testimonies against the Jews" 2.25, trans. Ernest Wallis, in *The Ante-Nicene Fathers*, 3:421–557, at 525.

11. P. Vielhauer, trans., "Jewish-Christian Gospels," in *New Testament*

Apocrypha, ed. Wilhelm Schneemelcher, English trans. George Ogg, English edition ed. R. M. Wilson (Philadelphia: Westminster, 1963), 117–65, esp. 148.

12. R. Hugh Connolly, trans., *Didascalia Apostolorum* 21 v. 13 (Oxford: Clarendon Press, 1929), 182.

13. Justin, *Dialogue with Trypho* 107.2, in *The Ante-Nicene Fathers*, 252; Gregory of Nazianzen, cited in R. H. Bowers, *The Legend of Jonah* (The Hague: Martinus Nijhoff, 1971), 31; Haymo of Halberstadt, John Calvin, and Martin Luther likewise cited in Bowers. My debt to Bowers's research, though not his analysis or conclusions, will be manifest to anyone familiar with his book, and I acknowledge it here.

14. Tyconius, *The Book of Rules*, trans. William S. Babcock, SBL Texts and Translations 31, Early Christian Literature Series (Atlanta: Scholars Press, 1989), 91–97. Cited in Bowers, *Legend of Jonah*, 45.

15. R. H. Gundry, *Matthew: A Commentary on His Literary and Theological Art* (Grand Rapids: Eerdmans, 1982), 244.

16. Martin Luther, *Lectures on the Minor Prophets II* (Jonah and Habakkuk), *Works* 19, trans. Jaroslav Pelikan, ed. H. C. Oswald (St. Louis: Concordia, 1974), 16.

17. Gundry, *Matthew*, 245.

18. S. Thelwall, trans., "A Strain of Jonah the Prophet," in *The Ante-Nicene Fathers* 3:150–52, at 152.

19. Irenaeus, "Against Heresies" 3.20.1, in *The Ante-Nicene Fathers* 1:315–567, at 450.

20. Methodius, "On the History of Jonah," trans. William R. Clark, in *The Ante-Nicene Fathers* 6:378.

21. Cited in Bowers, *Legend of Jonah*, 27–28.

22. Ibid., 26.

23. Ibid., 40.

24. Ibid.

25. B. W. Bacon, "What Was the Sign of Jonah?" *Biblical World* 20 (1902): 99–112.

26. Rudolf Bultmann, *The History of the Synoptic Tradition*, trans. John Marsh (New York: Harper & Row, 1963), 118.

27. Joachim Jeremias, "'Ιωνᾶς," in *Theological Dictionary of the New Testament* 3, trans. and ed. Geoffrey Bromiley (Grand Rapids: Eerdmans, 1965), 406–10; 409.

28. Ibid., 410.

29. John Howton, "The Sign of Jonah," *Scottish Journal of Theology* 15 (1962): 288–304.

30. Eugene H. Merrill, "The Sign of Jonah," *Journal of the Evangelical Theological Society* 23 (1980): 23–30.

31. George M. Landes, "Matthew 12:40 as an Interpretation of the 'Sign of Jonah' against Its Biblical Background," in Carol L. Myers, M.

O'Connor, eds., *The Word of the Lord Shall Go Forth: Essays in Honor of David Noel Freedman in Celebration of His Sixtieth Birthday* (special volume series/American Schools of Oriental Research (Winona Lake, Ind.: Eisenbrauns, 1983), 665–84; 676.

32. George M. Landes, "The Old Testament Background to the 'Sign of Jonah' Pericope in Luke 11:29–32" (lecture, annual meeting of the Society of Biblical Literature, Atlanta, 1986), 7.

33. Pierre Bonnard, *L'Évangile selon Saint Matthieu* (Neuchatel: Delachaux & Nièstle, 1970), 184n.

34. Walter Wink, *The Bible in Human Transformation* (Philadelphia: Fortress Press, 1973), 16–18; and Elizabeth Schüssler Fiorenza, *Bread Not Stone* (Boston: Beacon, 1984), 24.

CHAPTER 8

1. The two groups ought not be glibly identified as pro-gay (in the first case) and conservative-traditional (in the second case). Some gay Christians hold the second position and experience concomitant destructive self-loathing, while some straight Christians want to reserve the possibility of gratifying their carnal interests apart from theological justifications.

2. James Barr has defended the idea of natural theology in the Bible in his Gifford Lectures, published as *Biblical Faith and Natural Theology* (Oxford: Oxford University Press, 1993).

3. If we stipulate that *natural* means "scientifically verifiable," then arguments concerning "natural" sexuality cannot settle questions by appealing to Scripture any more than paleontologists can solve questions about dinosaurs by appealing to Genesis. But if we stipulate that *natural* means "according with what we take to be God's will," Paul's assessment of natural sexuality in Romans 1 can no more determine our perspective on what is natural than can his assessment of natural hairstyles in 1 Corinthians 11:14 or God's unnatural horticultural practices in Romans 11:24. Dale Martin has pointed out a number of grave interpretive problems with taking Romans 1 as the last word on natural human sexuality in "Heterosexism and the Interpretation of Romans 1:26–38" *Biblical Interpretation* 3 (1995): 332-55.

4. We should be alert to the fact that Old Testament marriage metaphors frequently take a dangerous tack, characterizing God as a spouse who, for a time, abandons Israel to brutal oppression in order to teach Israel a lesson, then returns when Israel has had enough. This is often the sort of rhetoric that human spouses parrot to justify spousal abuse, and we would be remiss if we soft-pedaled the damage that such abusive spouses can inflict in the name of God. In the interest to faithfulness to humanity and to God, we need to distinguish codependent abusiveness from genuine fidelity.

5. Katherine Doob Sakenfeld's *Faithfulness in Action*, Overtures to Biblical Theology (Philadelphia: Fortress Press, 1985), gives a thorough account of God's *hesed* (loyalty; covenant-faithfulness) that greatly enhances the premises of this essay.

6. No one should use a criterion of constancy as a cruel instrument of coercion to require that people who have fallen into destructive relationships eschew divorce, especially since the church that blessed and promised to support that relationship is implicated in the baneful relationship. If people enter into a marriage that they and their community come to see as unsalvageable, they should acknowledge that state of affairs and bring the relationship to an end. In such a case, not only the ex-spouses have failed; the congregation that gathered to witness the marriage, and that committed itself to do all in its power to uphold them in their marriage, shares the failure. The church should thus penitently recognize and compassionately share the pain that comes with acknowledging such an error in judgment, and should promptly act to embody God's reconciling love to divorced sisters and brothers. The church should not, however, take lightly this sign that the participants in the (former) marriage proved unable to live out the commitments they had made, and should be extremely cautious about supposing that the divorced parties have attained sufficient perspective on that misunderstanding to undertake again the commitments inherent in the vocation of Christian marriage. Also, the clergy and congregation should undertake careful self-examination to ascertain how they might have prevented such a regrettable end to the joyous beginning of the marriage.

7. Once again, Dale Martin makes a case that the term *natural* in first-century ethical discourse is perhaps best interpreted as "conventional." Martin, "Heterosexism and the Interpretation of Romans 1:18-32" (citing illuminating examples from the Hellenistic literature).

EPILOGUE

1. A. K. M. Adam, "Poaching on Zion: Biblical Theology as Signifying Practice" (Winslow Lecture, Seabury-Western Episcopal Seminary, Evanston, Ill., April 21, 2005), in A. K. M. Adam, Stephen E. Fowl, Kevin J. Vanhoozer, and Francis Watson, *Reading Scripture with the Church: Toward a Hermeneutic for Theological Interpretation* (Grand Rapids: Baker Academic, 2006), 17–34; "'Do This': Translating, Re-presenting, and Signifying New Testament Theology," (lecture, annual meeting of the Catholic Biblical Association, Collegeville, Minn., August 8, 2005).

2. My examination of de la Taille's eucharistic theology has been inhibited by time constraints and differences among editions of his work. David Jones cites this phrase in his essay "Art and Sacrament": "I venture to ask the reader to consider what Maurice de la Taille said

was done on Maundy Thursday by Good Friday's Victim, I quote: 'He placed Himself in the order of signs.'" In *Epoch and Artist*, ed. Harman Grisewood (London: Faber & Faber, 1959), 179. Jones does not cite the specific page of that quotation, but Christopher C. Knight, in "Some Liturgical Implications of the Thought of David Jones," *New Blackfriars* 85 (1998): 445, supplies what Jones did not, locating the phrase on p. 212 of *The Mystery of Faith and Human Opinion Contrasted and Defined*, trans. J. B. Schimpf (London: Sheed & Ward, 1930). David Blamires, in *David Jones: Artist and Writer* (Manchester: Manchester University Press, 1971), 29, explains that this is an English résumé of the complete work: *The Mystery of Faith*, vol. 1, *The Sacrifice of Our Lord* (New York: Sheed & Ward, 1940); and vol. 2, *The Sacrifice of the Church* (New York: Sheed & Ward, 1950). However, that seems a misleading characterization of what comprises a body of essays, letters, and outlines that complement but do not truly summarize the argument in the longer work. My intense thanks to Mary Ocasek of the Feehan Memorial Library of the University of St. Mary of the Lake for her help in tracking down the 1930 volume.

One cannot read de la Taille without observing the horrific anti-Judaism of his repeated emphatic charge of deicide against "the Jews." That misreading of the Passion and of God's relation to Israel casts a grim light on his eucharistic theology, but the point I draw from his writings does not in any way depend on blaming Jesus' neighbors for his execution, explicitly wrought by Roman authority.

3. Luke uses the word often for narrating (Luke 24:35; Acts 10:8; 15:12, 14; 21:19), and the related noun forms (*exēgētēs, exēgoria, exēgēsis*) appear in the LXX with senses related to narration. John is the only New Testament author other than Luke who uses these or related forms.

4. John Webster warns against ascribing an "incarnational" divine/human character to the biblical text in order to finesse problems of authority and error. *Holy Scripture: A Dogmatic Sketch* (Cambridge: Cambridge University Press, 2003), 22–23. My use of "incarnation" here avoids invoking an alleged Chalcedonian character of the biblical text, though it certainly may fall prey to other pitfalls.

5. In criticizing the posited necessity of historical-critical scholarship put forward by *The Interpretation of the Bible in the Church*, Stephen Fowl and Lewis Ayres point out, "Whereas Adam's claim is that historical criticism cannot protect christological orthodoxy, our argument is that christological orthodoxy cannot protect historical criticism." "(Mis)reading the Face of God: *The Interpretation of the Bible in the Church*," *Theological Studies* 60 (1999): 514 n. 4, referring to my argument in "Docetism, Käsemann, and Christology: Why Historical Criticism Can't Protect Christological Orthodoxy, *Scottish Journal of Theology* 49 (1996): 391–410 (chapter 2 in this volume).

6. "I shall call signifying practice the establishment and the counter-vailing of a sign system." From the glossary that Léon Roudiez appends to Julia Kristeva's *Desire in Language: A Semiotic Approach to Literature and Art* (New York: Columbia University Press, 1980), 18. Roudiez quotes from *La traversée des signes*, ed. Julia Kristeva et. al. (Paris: Sevil, 1975), without further specification. Roland Barthes makes illuminating use of Kristeva's distinction between phenotext and genotext in his essay "The Grain of the Voice," in *Image—Music—Text*, trans. Stephen Heath (New York: Hill & Wang, 1977), 179–89.

7. *The Kristeva Reader*, 120–23, citing *Revolution in Poetic Language*, ed. Toril Moi (New York: Columbia University Press, 1986).

8. Stuart Hall, ed., *Representation: Cultural Representations and Signify-ing Practices* (London: Sage, 1997), 15–64, esp. 28–29.

9. Dick Hebdige, *Subculture: The Meaning of Style* (London: Rout-ledge, 1979).

10. The preceding two paragraphs are drawn from my essay, "Poach-ing on Zion," in *Reading Scripture with the Church*.

11. Catherine Pickstock, *After Writing: On the Liturgical Consumma-tion of Philosophy*, Challenges in Contemporary Theology Series (Oxford: Blackwell, 1998), 253.

12. De la Taille, *The Mystery of Faith* (1930), 213.

13. Pickstock, *After Writing* xv, 261–64.

14. Maurice de la Taille, *The Mystery of Faith* (1930), 215.

15. Jones says this most prominently in "Art and Sacrament" and *Use and Sign* (Ipswich: Golgonooza, 1962).

16. Jones, *Use and Sign*, 7.

17. Jones applies this theme to more specifically liturgical observa-tions, which demand more thorough articulation than time permits for this paper. To apprehend the integration of liturgical semiosis with exegesis and theological reasoning, I read Jones beside Graham Hughes's *Worship as Meaning* (Cambridge: Cambridge University Press, 2003), with claims comparable to those Michael Bayldon advances in "Body-Language: Post Vatican II Liturgy," *New Blackfriars* 86 (2005): 450–53, only in conjunc-tion with the claims I make here about signifying practices.

18. The temptation to explore the semantics and implications of *monogene⁻s theos* (unique God or only-begotten God) beckons but must be resisted as peripheral to the point of this particular essay. What-ever we should make of that locution, John has identified the one who *exe⁻ge⁻tai* (explains) God as the Word who became flesh, and has com-pared Jesus' glory to that of a monogenous to a Father, so it seems safe to pursue my proposal on the premise that Jesus is the one who expounds the Father.

19. This is not, of course, a uniquely Johannine point; Matthew's Jesus likewise commands that disciples let their light so shine before all

people that they may see their good works and glorify the Father in heaven (5:16), and the Pauline imitation motif can serve this purpose (as in chapter 6, 105-23).

INDEX